LIPREADING FOR A MORE ACTIVE LIFE

By Mae T. Fisher

The Alexander Graham Bell Association for the Deaf, Inc.
3417 Volta Place, N.W., Washington, D.C. 20007, U.S.A.

Library of Congress Catalogue Card Number 76-55143

ISBN 0-88200-075-6

TABLE OF CONTENTS

TO THE READER:

These are revised lipreading lessons. In fact, they are a whole
new concept of ideas, as each lesson is a complete lesson in
itself. This makes it easier for home practice and, at the same
time, allows the classroom teacher plenty of leeway in adding to
or changing the material.

As an added bonus, an Alphabetical Listing of Homophenous Words
is included. These should be of great assistance in auditory
training and the teaching of speech and lipreading.

Lipreading should be interesting as well as helpful.

                                        Mae T. Fisher

LESSON 1--INITIAL M, P, B

Description: The lips come together, then open.

VOCABULARY

passport	money
breakfast	palm
banana	march
book	month
mile	paper
bicycle	post office

1. Do you have your passport with you?
2. That is a very good passport picture of you.

1. Shall we have waffles and bacon for breakfast?
2. We always have a late breakfast on Saturday.

1. These bananas are too ripe.
2. Some bananas are red, and some bananas are yellow.

1. Are you a member of the Book of the Month Club?
2. Where can I buy a book of proverbs?

1. We live one mile from the White House.
2. The last mile always seems the longest.

1. Many of my friends ride a bicycle to work.
2. My bicycle has a flat tire.

1. How much money is in the piggy bank?
2. Most of my money goes for groceries.

1. Would you rather live in Palm Beach or Miami?
2. The weather in Palm Beach is always warm.

1. Bob has a birthday in March.
2. The first day of March is on a Monday.

1. Where will you be one month from today?
2. We plan to spend a month in Miami.

1. Our paper boy is my big brother.
2. The paper boy rides a bicycle.

1. The post office is open from nine until five.
2. The main post office is on Pennsylvania Avenue.

HOMOPHENES

Procedure: Put one word from each group on the blackboard.

paperback

I paid $1.50 for this paperback book.
Please put the groceries in a brown <u>paperbag</u>.

met

Where have we met before?
Please be careful when you <u>pet</u> the dog.
This feather <u>bed</u> is too soft.
Please do not <u>bet</u> too much money on the ball game.
If you <u>bend</u> the plastic it will break.
Have you ever seen Big <u>Ben</u> in London?
May I borrow your ball point <u>pen</u>?
How long will it take to <u>mend</u> the chair?

my

This is my new phone number.
Who made this delicious pumpkin <u>pie</u>?
What time shall I stop <u>by</u> on Friday?
I did not see you wave "<u>bye</u>" to me.
We <u>buy</u> our shoes and our suits at the same shop.

be

What time will you be home for lunch?
A <u>bee</u> was buzzing around my head.
I thought I heard someone speak to <u>me</u>.
We will have cream of <u>pea</u> soup for supper.

bear

Where does the polar bear live?
Please give me just the <u>bare</u> facts.
The <u>pear</u> tree has white blossoms.
I need a new <u>pair</u> of walking shoes.

DESCRIPTIVE DEVICE--FAMOUS BIRTHPLACES

Procedure: Read for thought.   Have pupil repeat as much as he followed.

This birthplace is in the south.
It is in a small town in Alabama.
This is the hometown of a famous deaf and blind person.
This is the birthplace of Helen Keller.

This birthplace is in the south.
The place was a small log cabin.
The man became our sixteenth President.
This is the birthplace of Abraham Lincoln.

This birthplace is far away.
It is in a small city in Italy.
The city is Genoa.
This is the birthplace of Christopher Columbus.

This birthplace is up north in Michigan.
It is the home of a national hero.
He was the first one to fly solo across the Atlantic.
This is the birthplace of Charles Lindbergh.

This birthplace is in Pennsylvania.
It is the home of a famous poet.
We remember him for the words "barefoot boy with cheeks of tan."
This is the birthplace of James Whitcomb Riley.

This birthplace is in the south.
This place is in New Orleans, Louisiana.
It is the home of a famous musician.
This is the birthplace of Louis Armstrong.

This birthplace is far away.
It is in a small town in France.
A President of France once lived here.
This is the birthplace of Charles DeGaulle.

This birthplace is up north.
It is in the State of Maine.
This man was a poet.
This is the birthplace of Henry Wadsworth Longfellow.

This birthplace is far away.
This place is in Haiti.
This man loved birds.
This is the birthplace of James Audubon.

This birthplace is in the south.
It is in Shreveport, Louisiana.
It is the birthplace of a famous pianist.
This is the birthplace of Van Cliburn.

This is the birthplace of a Nobel Prize winner.
This place is in the foothills of the Allegheny mountains.
She was a famous woman writer.
This is the birthplace of Pearl Buck.

LESSON 2--F, V, PH, AND FINAL GH

Description: These consonants have the same formation. The lower lip is against the upper teeth.

VOCABULARY

food	visit
feel	valley
five	have
far	enough
voice	laugh
vacation	chief

1. What is your favorite food?
2. The Safeway is having a sale on breakfast food.

1. How do you feel today?
2. Do you feel like going for a three-mile hike?

1. My vacation was five weeks ago.
2. We spent the first five days in France.

1. How far did you go on your vacation?
2. We did not go as far as we had planned to go.

1. My father-in-law has a very low voice.
2. His voice sounds more like a woman's voice than a man's voice.

1. Our vacation was too short.
2. Why do most people take their vacation in the summer?

1. I would like to visit some old friends in Florida.
2. We plan to visit in Memphis on our way south.

1. My favorite flower is lily of the valley.
2. A heavy fog hung over the valley.

1. We have a surprise for you.
2. We have been saving the surprise for your birthday.

1. We have more than enough ice cream for everyone.
2. Are you sure that there is enough for fifty people?

1. Laugh and the world laughs with you.
2. The doctor says we should laugh more often.

1. The chief of police lives across the street.
2. The chief of police is six foot five inches tall.

HOMOPHENES

Procedure: Put one word from each group on the blackboard.

fad
Do you follow the latest fad?
We will stew the <u>fat</u> chicken and make dumplings.
There is a draft from the electric <u>fan</u>.
The moving <u>van</u> is due at nine o'clock.

fair
She tries to be fair to everyone.
What is the <u>fare</u> on the Metroliner from Washington to New York?

few
We need a few more names on the list.
Do you listen to the program called "The <u>View</u> From
    Capitol Hill"?

fur
This is my favorite fake fur.
How far south does the <u>fir</u> tree grow?

phone
The man from the phone company is due this morning.
Please do not do anything to lose your <u>vote</u>.

verse
Almost everyone knows the first verse of "Home on the Range."
Is this the <u>first</u> time you have driven a Volkswagen?

vase
The vase was made of Steuben glass.
Why didn't <u>phase</u> four work out as planned?
Please <u>face</u> this way when you speak to me.

vital
It is wrong to withhold vital information.
The <u>final</u> decision is up to the president.

vine
The first grape vine came from Spain.
You may pay the <u>fine</u> by mail.

very
That is a very interesting question.
Some restaurants never seem to <u>vary</u> their Friday menus.
The <u>ferry</u> leaves the wharf at seven-fifteen five mornings
    a week.

QUESTIONS AND ANSWERS ON VALLEY FORGE

Procedure: There are two ways to present this device. The teacher
may give the question and then the answer herself, or she
may ask the question and have a pupil standing beside her
read the answer. This makes for good class participation.

Where is Valley Forge?
    Valley Forge is in beautiful Pennsylvania.

Why is the year 1777 to 1778 associated with Valley Forge?
> That is the year which George Washington and his men spent at Valley Forge.

How many men did Washington have in his army at this time?
> He had 11,000 men.

How many men were fit for duty?
> Only two-thirds were fit for duty.

In what month of the year did the army arrive at Valley Forge?
> They arrived in December, but it was January before all of the men had a roof over their heads.

What kind of houses did the men live in?
> The men lived in log huts.

When did Washington move into his stone house?
> Washington moved in on Christmas Eve.

Who joined Washington and lived in the house with him?
> Martha joined him on February 10th and stayed until June 8th.

What kind of a winter did the men have?
> They had a long cold winter in which 3,000 men died.

Can you name some well-known men who were on Washington's staff?
> Some of the men were Henry Knox, Alexander Hamilton, John Marshall, James Madison, and James Monroe.

What famous French general aided Washington?
> This was General Lafayette, who was a good friend of General Washington.

LESSON 3--INITIAL S

Description: Teeth come together for "s."

VOCABULARY

same	soap
salt	sell
seem	seven
sofa	September
sage	something
soup	sandalwood
sun	

1. Some people spend their vacations at the same place each year.
2. We have had the same telephone number for years.

1. Do you use garlic salt?
2. The recipe calls for one half teaspoon of salt.

1. It seems to me there is a mistake in this bill.
2. Does this place seem familiar to you?

1. Have you ever had to sleep on the sofa?
2. Please put the box on the sofa.

1. Sometimes the leaves of the sage plant are gray.
2. Did you know that sage is used in medicine?

1. What is the soup of the day?
2. The soup of the day is oxtail soup.

1. Do you believe there is nothing new under the sun?
2. When the sun shines in my eyes it gives me a headache.

1. This soap has a nice clean smell.
2. This soap comes in three sizes.

1. We hope to sell the house at a profit.
2. Would you advise me to sell now or wait awhile?

1. Some shops are open seven days a week.
2. There were seven sisters in my mother's family.

1. The month of September is an ideal time to take a vacation.
2. Sometimes the weather can be very warm in September.

1. There is something in my eye.
2. May I bring you something from MacDonald's?

1. The box smells of sandalwood and spice.
2. This sandalwood box was made in Hawaii.

HOMOPHENES

Put one word from each group on the blackboard.

sense   That statement does not make sense.
                 Ten cents plus fifteen cents is twenty-five cents.
                 The toilet water comes in five different scents.
                 She sends all of her packages by special delivery.

serve   Shall we serve red wine or white wine with the dinner?
                 We could hear the roar of the surf from our hotel window.

straight   There were four straight lines on the paper.
                 Who named the Strait of Gibraltar?

slip   If we slip the head waiter a good tip he will get us a
                    good table.
                 Was Thomas Jefferson our first tall, slim President?

slam   We heard the garage door slam as the wind blew it shut.
                 I found this slab of marble in an old shop in Georgetown.
                 I saw you slap that mosquito.

sand   The sand storm lasted for days.
                 We sat on a rock and rested our feet.
                 It is difficult to be sad on such a beautiful day.

DESCRIPTIVE DEVICE--CITIES

Procedure: Read the entire description for thought.

This is a medium size city.
This city is in the east.
The city was famous for witchcraft.
This is Salem, Massachusetts.

This city is in Maryland.
This city is in Montgomery County.
This city is not far from Washington.
This is Silver Spring, Maryland.

This city is in the south.
There are many beautiful flowers in this city.
The weather is warm here most of the time.
This is Savannah, Georgia.

This city is in the west.
This city is not too far from Hollywood.
This city is the capital of the state.
This is Sacramento, California.

This city is in the southwest.
It is one of the oldest cities in the United States.
This city has the same name as a famous railroad.
This is Santa Fe, New Mexico.

This city is in the south.
It is a very old city.
There are many quaint old buildings here.
This is St. Augustine, Florida.

This city is in the midwest.
The people here are very friendly.
Most of the people are Mormons.
This is Salt Lake City, Utah.

This city is in the south.
It is in the southwestern part of its state.
Although it is small, it is very much in the news.
This is the home of our thirty-eighth President.
This is Plains, Georgia.

LESSON 4--SOFT C

Description: Soft C has the same formation as "s." The teeth come together,
then open.

VOCABULARY

cent

cigarette

city

cigar

celery

celebrate

census

cereal

certain

certify

cinnamon

civil

Cincinnati

ceiling

1. Whose picture is on the ten-cent stamp?
2. This two-cent stamp is worth ten dollars.

1. Do you believe that cigarette smoking is harmful?
2. When was the last time you saw a cigarette ad on TV?

1. We live five miles from the nearest city.
2. What is the present population of New York City?

1. Do you like the smell of a good cigar?
2. Winston Churchill loved to smoke a good cigar.

1. Do we buy celery by the bunch or by the pound?
2. There are many celery farms in Florida.

1. Do you always celebrate your birthday?
2. Let's celebrate with a big party on Friday night.

1. Who is the director of the census bureau?
2. When was the first census taken?

1. Mr. Post made a fortune with his cereal.
2. There are many brands of cereal on the market.

1. Are you certain you gave me the key to the door?
2. I am certain that is the same man we saw Saturday.

1. The bank will certify the check for you.
2. The certified check was worth five thousand dollars.

1. Shall we have coffee and hot cinnamon rolls for brunch?
2. There is too much cinnamon in the apple pie.

10

1. When did you take your Civil Service exam?
2. Are you a Civil War buff?

1. What is the population of Cincinnati?
2. Cincinnati is across the river from Louisville.

1. Some old homes have high ceilings.
2. The ceiling in my room needs to be painted.

HOMOPHENES

Procedure: Put one word from each group on the blackboard.

ceiling   Shall we paint the ceiling a light blue?
              Who wrote a poem about sealing wax and kings?

cent   What is the date on the twenty-five cent piece?
              I sent John to the drugstore for aspirin.
              We said the same things but used different words.

cite   Some people can cite Scripture at the drop of a hat.
              Please keep in sight so we will not lose you.
              The "for sale" sign in front of the house is gone.

center   The table was in the center of the room.
              We will mark the letter "return to sender."

DESCRIPTIVE DEVICE

Soft "C" Words

Procedure: Paragraph is read for thought.

This is a piece of paper.
It is small.
It is square.
It has a picture on one side.
We put this on mail.
This is a one-cent stamp.

This thing is long.
It is green.
It crawls.
It has many feet.
It is supposed to have 100 feet.
This is a centipede.

This is long and round.
It can be fat.
It can be thin.
It is brown.
Sometimes it smells good.
Sometimes it smells terrible.
This is a cigar.

This is a liquid.
It is brown.
Sometimes it is sweet.
Sometimes it is sour.
This is made from apples.
This is cider.

It can be round.
It can be oval.
It can be green.
It can be orange.
It grows on a tree.
This is a citrus fruit.

This is round.
It can be long and thin.
It can be short and thin.
It is white.
Both men and women smoke this.
This is a cigarette.

This is a spice.
It is brown.
It is made from the bark of a tree.
It has a nice smell.
It tastes good.
This is cinnamon.

This can be small.
Sometimes it is so small we do not see it.
But we know it is there.
It can be brown or black.
It hurts if it gets into our eyes.
This is a cinder.

This is a vegetable.
Sometimes it is green.
Sometimes it is white.
We can cook this.
We can eat it raw in a salad.
It grows in stalks.
This is celery.

This is a tree.
It grows in the south.
The wood is valuable.
A branch of this tree is an emblem of mourning.
This is the cypress tree.

LESSON 5--INITIAL SH

Description: For the formation of "sh" the lips form somewhat of a square.

VOCABULARY

shampoo	shower
ship	she
shrimp	shoulder
shoe	shadow
share	Shasta
shot	Shakespeare

1. Wouldn't you love to have hair like the girls in the shampoo ads?
2. Have you ever tried a shampoo tint on your hair?

1. If you ship your furniture by rail you must crate the furniture.
2. Would you rather cross the ocean by ship or by plane?

1. There are shrimp and crab cakes on the seafood platter.
2. Louisiana is famous for its shrimp.

1. The horse shoe is a sign of good luck.
2. I found this old horse shoe in the stable.

1. The first prize was two shares of General Motors stock.
2. How much was your share of the estate?

1. Who fired the first shot heard round the world?
2. Some people react to a flu shot.

1. The weather man predicts showers for tomorrow.
2. Most of our showers are early in the morning.

1. She is my friend.
2. Why is a ship called a "she"?

1. We all need someone's shoulder to cry on.
2. You can depend upon him to shoulder his share of the responsibility.

1. The puppy plays with his shadow.
2. Have you ever tried to make shadow pictures on the wall?

1. There is always snow on the top of Mt. Shasta.
2. We had a good view of Mt. Shasta from the train window.

1. How old was Shakespeare when he died?
2. The Shakespearean festival is held every summer.

HOMOPHENES

Procedure: Put one word from each group on the blackboard.

show   Who played in the movie "Show Boat"?
That fellow seems like a good <u>Joe</u>.

shot   Mary was a crack shot on the Olympic rifle team.
<u>John</u> is in his first year of college.
Will you <u>jot</u> down any ideas you may have?

shore   The ship went down in sight of shore.
It was a <u>chore</u> for me to get started on the ironing.

shack   The hunters spent the night in a shack in the woods.
Let's play the game with the <u>Jack</u> of Spades wild.

shade   That is an odd shade of green.
Where can you buy good <u>jade</u>?
<u>Jane</u> is five years older than John.

DESCRIPTIVE DEVICE--SOMETHING AROUND THE HOUSE

Procedure: Read for thought. Then ask questions.

This can be large or small.
It can be open or closed.
It can be straight or oblong.
It can be very sharp or very dull.
Everyone uses this.
It is one of the first things we wear as babies.

                                                  Pin

This is small.
Sometimes it is so small we do not see it.
But we know it is there.
We use it to season our food.
Sometimes it is red and sometimes it is black.
Sometimes it makes us sneeze.

                                                Pepper

This can be large, medium sized, or small.
It can be any shape.
It is waterproof.
It has many uses.
It is made of plastic.
It is especially useful in the kitchen.
We can put leftover food in this and store it in the refrigerator.

Plastic bag or bowl

This is a very important item in the home.
It can be large or small.
It can be fragile or heavy.
It can be fancy or plain.
We use it many times a day.
Sometimes it is the first thing we use in the morning.
Sometimes it is the last thing we use at night.
We drink out of this.

Coffee cup

This can be small, medium sized, or large.
It can be round, square, or oval.
It can lay flat on a table.
It can be propped up on a dresser.
It can hang on a wall or it can be fastened to a door.
It is a very important item in the home.
This tells us how we look.

Mirror

This can be large or small.
It can be heavy or light.
It can be made of steel or plastic.
It can be found in the bedroom.
It can be found in a man's pocket.
It can be found in a lady's handbag.
Almost everyone uses this.
We fix our hair with this.

Comb

This can be large or small.
We use this in the kitchen.
It is on the kitchen shelf.
But most of the time we find this in the bathroom.
It is on the bathroom floor.
Some people like this.
Some people dislike this.
This one in the bathroom tells us when we should go on a diet.

Scales

This is smaller than a breadbox.
But it is just as important.
Sometimes it is made of tin.
Sometimes it is made of ceramic china.
We find this on a kitchen shelf.
It is filled with sweet things to eat.
Children love to raid this.

                                        Cookie Jar

This can be large or small.
It can be used by hand.
It can be run by electricity.
Men and women both use this.
This is found in the kitchen.
No cook should be without one.
A bride especially likes this.

                                        Can Opener

This can be large or small.
But it is usually medium sized.
It is generally made of glass.
It has markings on the side.
Not every home has one.
But most modern homes have one.
We use this for mixing drinks.

                                        Cocktail Shaker

This can be large or small.
It can be made of glass or china.
It is very important in many homes.
Men and women both use this.
This helps keep ashes off the floor.

                                        Ash Tray

LESSON 6--INITIAL CH

Description: "Ch" has the same formation as "Sh"--the lips form somewhat
of a square.

VOCABULARY

charge

church

chart

child

china

chimney

chess

cheese

chili

chopsticks

Chippendale

chocolate

chapter

1.   Someone has been using my charge-a-plate.
2.   I lost my charge plate when I was shopping last Wednesday.

1.   Tom Thumb was married in the Little Church Around the Corner.
2.   The Little Church Around the Corner is in New York City.

1.   The first charts were made of papyrus.
2.   A chart is a map of the sea.

1.   She is just a child of nature.
2.   Have you ever tried any of Julia Child's recipes?

1.   Would you like to visit mainland China?
2.   Are China and Japan friends again?

1.   The chimney stack was damaged by the storm.
2.   The chimney sweep is a brush with a long handle.

1.   Who is the chess champion of the world?
2.   The game of chess requires deep concentration.

1.   This jar of cheddar cheese came from Wisconsin.
2.   Will you grate the cheese for the fondue?

1.   Have you tried my new recipe for chili?
2.   I like plenty of ground meat in my chili.

1.   Have you ever learned to eat Chinese food with chopsticks?
2.   These ivory chopsticks came from China.

1.   The antiques shop specializes in Chippendale furniture.
2.   Charlotte is a collector of Chippendale furniture.

1. Chocolate is made from the nut of the cacao tree.
2. This dark Swiss chocolate is very rich.

1. There were only fourteen chapters in the book.
2. We were disappointed in the last chapter.

HOMOPHENES

chew   The puppy will chew your shoe if you let him.
I found one shoe under the bed and the other in the closet.

choose   Will you choose the day best for you?
These shoes are very comfortable.

chain   Who sent you the chain letter?
Let's rest for a while in the shade.

choir   Did you ever sing in a church choir?
There are 24 sheets in a quire of paper.

cheap   We are looking for a good cheap typewriter.
The first Jeep was made in Pennsylvania.

DESCRIPTIVE DEVICE--PARAGRAPHS FOR THOUGHT

Procedure: Read through sentence by sentence; then re-read
             quickly as a paragraph.

1.   This man was born in 1808.
     He was born in New Hampshire.
     His folks moved around a lot.
     They moved from one state to another.
     He went to law school.
     The first place he practiced law was in Washington, D.C.
     Later on he practiced law in Ohio.
     He became a U.S. Senator from 1849-1855.
     From 1856 to 1860 he was Governor of Ohio.
     He was a very intelligent man.
     He laid out the basis of our present banking system.
     He was Secretary of the Treasury under Abraham Lincoln.
     Later on he was appointed Chief Justice by Lincoln.
     He had another very important job.
     He presided over the impeachment trial of Andrew Johnson.
     This man was Solomon P. Chase.

2.   This is a city.
     It is a capital city.
     It is a very interesting city.
     The city is surrounded by water.
     The city has a large harbor.
     The city is on an island in the Caribbean.
     The island is 40 miles east of Puerto Rico.
     The city is famous as a tourist resort.
     It has been called a "shoppers' paradise."
     The city was named for a princess.
     The princess was the wife of King Christian V of Denmark.
     The city is Charlotte Amalie.

LESSON 7--INITIAL AND MEDIAL SOFT G

Description: Soft G has the same formations as "Sh" and "Ch." The lips
form somewhat of a square.

VOCABULARY

gem	geography
giraffe	generous
gypsy	Geneva
George	baggage
geranium	angel
ginger	pigeon

1. The ruby is a more valuable gem than the emerald.
2. What is one of the most valuable gems in the world?

1. Does the giraffe have large feet or small feet?
2. The monkey loves to tease the giraffe.

1. The gypsy has black hair and dark eyes.
2. The gypsy loves to wander from place to place.

1. Was Henry VIII as famous as King George IV?
2. Many famous people have been named George.

1. This geranium plant was grown in a hothouse.
2. The roots of geranium plants are used in some medicines.

1. Where does the ginger plant grow?
2. The ginger has a very spicy flavor.

1. The geography class has gone on a field trip.
2. The geography of the world is constantly changing.

1. You are too generous with your money.
2. I am more generous with my time than with my money.

1. Geneva is a beautiful city in Switzerland.
2. Many international conferences are held in Geneva.

1. How many pieces of baggage do you have with you?
2. We had to pay a five dollar excess baggage fee.

1. What are the colors of the angel fish?
2. The angel fish is found in the Atlantic Ocean.

1. There are too many pigeons in Washington.
2. The pigeon is a pest.

DESCRIPTIVE DEVICE

Soft G

Procedure: Read paragraph for thought. Ask questions.

This is a place.
It can be large or small.
It has a hard waxed floor.
Every school has one.
People exercise here.
Games are played here.   Gym

This is a person.
He is a very happy person.
He loves color.
He loves to travel.
He claims to know how to predict the future.   Gypsy

This is a plant.
It is an indoor plant.
Sometimes it is grown in a hothouse.
Sometimes it is grown in a pot in the home.
It has pink or red flowers.
Sometimes the leaves of the plant are used in medicine.   Geranium

This is something valuable.
Sometimes it is rare.
It can be any color.
It can be any shape.
It is usually found in the ground.
Then it is cleaned and polished.   Gem

This is something useful.
It is a unit of measure.
We use this to measure liquids.
It equals one fourth of a pint.   Gill

This is a person.
It can be a man or a woman.
This is a very important person.
This person holds a high office.
This person is connected with the Armed Services. General

This is a city.
It is a medium sized city.
This city is in Italy.
It was the home town of a famous man.
It was the home of Columbus   Genoa

This is a science.
This is the science of the surface of the earth.
This is the science of the earth's physical features.
It is the science of the earth's inhabitants.
It affects everyone.   Geography

This is something small.
It is something alive.
We can hardly see it.
The doctor sees it under a microscope.
This causes a lot of trouble.
This causes disease.   Germ

This is motion.
It can be a motion of the face.
It can be a motion of the body.
It can be a motion of the arms.
It can express emotion.
Or it can illustrate something that has been said.
Sometimes it is very dramatic.   Gesture

This is a plant.
This plant is noted for its smell.
It has a pungent smell.
It has a spicy taste.
Sometimes it is used in cooking.
It can be used in medicine.   Ginger

This is a plant.
This plant belongs to the herb family.
The root of the plant has a sharp taste.
The Chinese consider this a valuable herb.
The Chinese use it as medicine.   Ginseng

LESSON 8--W

Description: The lips are forward for the "w" formation, somewhat like
the long "oo" formation.

VOCABULARY

warm	wallpaper
watch	ways
waves	Washington
wax	Webster
weeds	wing
west	witness
wall	woman

1. Warm Springs, Georgia, is seventy miles southwest of Atlanta.
2. Warm Springs is famous for its mineral waters.

1. The first watches were made in Germany and France.
2. The patent for the first self-winding watch was taken out in 1780.

1. Some waves are formed by the wind.
2. Tidal waves are caused by the forces of the sun and the moon.

1. Most wax figures are made of beeswax.
2. The Egyptians used wax figures in their funeral rites.

1. Some weeds have beautiful flowers.
2. The rag weed is native to North America.

1. The West Indies are divided into two groups.
2. Cuba is the largest island of the West Indies.

1. The wailing wall is in the old city of Jerusalem.
2. The old wailing wall is a historic as well as religious site.

1. The use of wallpaper came to us from Europe.
2. Wallpaper was once known as paper tapestry.

1. Who is Chairman of the House Ways and Means Committee?
2. There are more ways than one to solve this problem.

1. George Washington's father went to school in England.
2. Washington's father died when Washington was only 11 years old.

1. Daniel Webster was born in New Hampshire in 1782.
2. Daniel Webster practiced law in Boston, Massachusetts.

1. What color are the wings of the blue jay?
2. The bird could not fly with a broken wing.

1. You may call your next witness.
2. Have you ever been a witness to a serious accident?

1. Can you give me the name of the new woman's magazine?
2. The woman refused to give her age and her weight.

HOMOPHENES

Procedure: Write one word from each group on the board.

wash
: We will wash the car on Saturday morning.
Please <u>watch</u> your step when you leave the bus.

were
: Where were you this time last year?
We could hear the <u>whir</u> of the machinery in the factory.

which
: The traffic officer will show you which way to go.
The <u>witch</u> rode a broom.
Did you ever <u>wish</u> you were someone else?

wad
: Please throw that wad of paper in the wastebasket.
<u>What</u> did you say?
The witch has a magic <u>wand</u>.

weak
: Why was the coffee so weak this morning?
Do you go to the movies more than once a <u>week</u>?

wait
: Everyone had to wait for the bus this morning.
We had to <u>wade</u> through water up to our ankles.
Some people need to gain <u>weight,</u> not lose.

win
: We always play to win.
Henry Kissinger is not the soul of <u>wit</u>.
The walk up the hill took the <u>wind</u> out of me.

white
: The boys have a white rabbit for a pet.
Pennsylvania Avenue is a very <u>wide</u> avenue.
I forgot to <u>wind</u> the grandfather clock.
Why do the puppies <u>whine</u> so much?
We prefer the white <u>wine</u> to the red wine.

QUESTIONS AND ANSWERS

Procedure: Seat pupils in semicircle and give them cards on which answers to questions have been written. Teacher gives the vocabulary word and then asks the question. The person having correct card answers.

wish   What more would you wish for if you had a million dollars?
There is nothing more I could wish for.

watch   Where did you find this old watch?
I found the old watch with my grandfather's things in a trunk in the attic.

white   Are the White Mountains in New Hampshire or Vermont?
The White Mountains are in New Hampshire.

work   Would you rather work for a Senator or a Congressman?
I think it would be more interesting to work for a Congressman.

walk   How far can you walk in one hour?
I don't know--I have never timed myself.

whisper   How far away can you hear a whisper?
Sometimes I can hear a whisper four feet away, and sometimes I cannot hear a whisper at all.

west   How far west have you traveled?
We have been as far west as Phoenix, Arizona.

wharf   What time does the ferry leave the wharf?
The ferry leaves the wharf every morning at seven on the dot.

way   Why do some people always expect to have their own way?
I don't know, I guess they are just selfish.

wait   Did you ever wait on tables at a church supper?
Yes, I do this once a month.

whippoorwill What kind of a song does the whippoorwill sing?
The whippoorwill sings a sad song.

Washington What profession did George Washington follow when he was sixteen years old?
He was a surveyor when he was sixteen years old.

Wyoming What sport did you see while you were in Wyoming?
We saw a cowboy roping a cow at a rodeo.

LESSON 9--INITIAL R

Description: For R at the beginning of the word, the lips pucker at
the corners and come forward.

VOCABULARY

read	real
rest	road
rich	rice
rough	Richmond
room	Revere
rush	Ruth

1. Will you read her letter to me?
2. Do you prefer to read the morning paper or the evening paper?

1. My head aches; I think I will lie down and rest for awhile.
2. Let's rest for ten minutes.

1. Everyone wishes they had a rich uncle.
2. Some rich people are very stingy.

1. Do your hands get chapped and rough in the winter?
2. The road was rough and there were lots of rocks in the road.

1. I do not have room in my bag for these shoes.
2. Are you sure there is room for one more?

1. I like to get up early so I will not have to rush.
2. The rush hour traffic will soon be over.

1. These artificial flowers look almost real.
2. We were in for a real surprise.

1. The Romans were the greatest road builders of all times.
2. The first great Roman road was built in 312 B.C.

1. A rice plant grows about four feet tall.
2. Rice has been grown since 3000 B.C.

1. Richmond is one hundred miles south of Washington.
2. The capital building at Richmond was designed by Jefferson.

1. Paul Revere's house still stands in Boston.
2. Paul Revere's father was French.

1. Ruth was the great-grandmother of David.
2. Is the Book of Ruth in the Old Testament or the New Testament?

HOMOPHENES

Procedure: Write one word from each group on the blackboard.

read   Do you read at night before you go to sleep?
       The porch furniture was made of <u>reed</u>.

write   Can you write with your left hand?
       My <u>right</u> ear is better than my left ear.
       Do you like to <u>ride</u> in the rain?
       The <u>Rhine</u> river is not a long river.

run   We saw a deer run through the woods.
       Our puppy is the <u>runt</u> of the litter.
       The car was stuck in the <u>rut</u>.

road   The road led to an old farmhouse.
       I <u>wrote</u> the name on the back of an old envelope.
       We <u>rode</u> through the pouring rain for three hours.
       The <u>Rhone</u> river is in France.
       A small boy <u>rowed</u> the big boat out onto the lake.

red   That is a very cheerful shade of red.
       How long will the <u>rent</u> freeze be in effect?
       The house <u>wren</u> is a small bird.

reside   Dr. Raymond plans to reside in Richmond.
       If you <u>resign</u> your job you will lose your pension.

reviews These book reviews come out once a month.
       If you <u>refuse</u> the gifts you will hurt his feelings.

rays   The rays of the setting sun brightened the room.
       How many times a year do you expect a pay <u>raise</u>?

QUESTIONS AND ANSWERS

Procedure: Give cards to pupils with R words underlined. Teacher
gives vocabulary word and then asks a question.
Whoever has correct answer reads to class.

rose   What is the name of your favorite rose?
My favorite rose is the Mamie Eisenhower rose.

Rhine   Where is the Rhine River?
The Rhine River is in Germany.

remember   What do you remember most about your childhood?
I remember the summers we spent on the farm.

radio   Did you hear the news first on radio or TV?
I heard the news first on the radio late last night.

rice   Do you have a good recipe for Spanish rice?
Yes, my Spanish rice recipe came from my mother.

run   Which can run faster, the jack rabbit or the
cottontail rabbit?
The jack rabbit can run faster.

reach   Can you reach the book on the top shelf?
No, I cannot reach it. I will have to get the stepladder.

rich   Which is the richest family in the United States?
The Mellon family is the richest family.

road   Does this road lead over to the main highway?
No, this road leads to the beach.

raspberry   Is the black raspberry sweeter than the red raspberry?
No, the red raspberry is the sweetest.

Rome   What did you do while you were in Rome?
We walked up the Spanish steps while we were in Rome.

Rochester   What large hospital is in Rochester, New York?
The Mayo Brothers Clinic is in Rochester, New York.

rhubarb   How many calories are there in a pound of rhubarb?
There are less calories in rhubarb than any other vegetable.

rodeo   What is a rodeo?
A rodeo is a series of cowboy contests.

row   What row are our seats in?
We have four front row seats for the show.

LESSON 10--FINAL R

Description: For R at the end of a word, the lips will pucker at the corner.
Difficult to see.

VOCABULARY

pour
: Will you pour the coffee while I cut the cake?
Please pour me a glass of milk.

sour
: Do you find this grapefruit unusually sour?
What shall we do with the sour milk?

hour
: They will be here in a quarter of an hour.
Do you have a favorite hour of the day?

better
: We could do a better job if we had more time.
Johnny promised to try to do better in his arithmetic.

pear
: Would you like a pear for dessert?
There was an apple and a pear in my lunch box.

share
: Will you share the taxi with me?
Bob will share the cake with his friend Johnny.

fire
: There was a big fire in the block where we live.
A fire broke out in a vacant warehouse.

summer
: Do you have any plans for next summer?
We always plan our summer vacation in December.

year
: We had a big snowstorm this time last year.
This time next year we will be in Mexico.

wore
: The boys wore their snow jackets to school today.
I wore my rain boots but it did not rain.

river
: Have you ever seen the lost river at Natural Bridge, Virginia?
Most rivers flow into an ocean or another river.

reindeer
: Both male and female reindeer have antlers.
The female reindeer has small antlers.

roadrunner
: The roadrunner spends most of its time running around looking
for food.
The tail of the roadrunner is as long as its body.

regular
: There were 776 men in the first regular army.
The club will have regular monthly meetings.

HOMOPHENES

Final R

Procedure: Write one word from each group on the blackboard.

fair
    Where will the next World's Fair be held?
    The airlines were not allowed to raise their <u>fare</u>.

wear
    Most uniforms are made of wash-and-wear material.
    This is the place <u>where</u> the pickpocket lifted my wallet.

summer
    It was such a short summer.
    The church <u>supper</u> was a success moneywise.

Parker
    The Parker House is an old Chicago landmark.
    Will you buy me a felt <u>marker</u> at the dime store?

sitter
    The baby sitter was late this evening.
    Mary Magdalene was a famous <u>sinner</u>.

air
    There was an air of suspense in the courtroom.
    Tiny Tim is very proud of his long <u>hair</u>.

near
    We heard a gun shot in the woods near the highway.
    The sign by the road says, "Careful, <u>Deer</u> Crossing."

DESCRIPTIVE DEVICE--WHO IS THIS MAN?

Procedure: Go around the class sentence by sentence, then re-read the
paragraph for thought.

He was born in Limoges, France, in 1841.
When he was very young he showed a talent for drawing.
He did not seem to like this.
Instead he began to paint window shades and fans in Paris.
He continued to study art in a studio.
There he met a man by the name of Monet.
They became good friends.
Monet later became famous.
In 1870 this man began to paint portraits.
He painted many portraits of wealthy people.
In 1880 he went to Italy to study art.
Later he returned to France.
In 1881 he painted a famous picture that now hangs in a museum in
   Washington.
This painting is called "The Luncheon of the Boating Party."
His paintings seem to be happy paintings.
They do not show the agony he suffered.
He had arthritis very badly.
His hands were crippled.
He could not hold a paint brush.
The brushes had to be tied to his hands.
He developed a style all of his own.
He used broad brush strokes and vivid colors.
He is famous for painting young girls and children.
He died in 1919.
This is Renoir.

LESSON 11--TH*

Description: For "th" the tongue is between the front teeth.

VOCABULARY

thunder	thread
thief	thrush
thimble	thyme*
thirteen	Thames*
thirty	Thailand*
thistle	third
Thomas*	

1. Long ago people were afraid of thunder.
2. Thursday is named for the God of Thunder.

1. What is the difference between a thief and a burglar?
2. A burglar is a thief who forces entrance into a building.

1. Mary, Queen of Scots, used a silver thimble.
2. Thimbles were used by the Chinese at a very early date.

1. Which was the first of the thirteen original states?
2. The last of the thirteen original states was Georgia.

1. The Thirty Years War was from 1618 to 1648.
2. The Thirty Years War involved eight countries.

1. The thistle is a common flower in Europe.
2. The golden thistle is used as a vegetable in some places.

1. Thomas is another name for twin.
2. Danny Thomas is a well-known TV comedian.

1. The first modern thread was used in England in 1754.
2. I keep a needle and thread at the office.

1. A thrush can grow to be one foot long.
2. Most birds of the thrush family are very good singers.

1. Thyme has a small pale lilac flower.
2. Thyme is the favorite food of bees.

1. The Thames is the second longest river in England.
2. Many famous sports events are held on the Thames River.

1. Thailand means the Land of the Free.
2. Thailand was called Siam from 1945 to 1949.

1. Tuesday is the third day of the week.
2. This is the third holiday we have had since Christmas.

* Four "th" words on this list are pronounced as the letter "t"

HOMOPHENES

"Two in One" Sentences

Procedure: Write one word on the board. Have the pupil watch for the
other word in the sentence that looks like the word on the board.

choose   You should choose your <u>shoes</u> with care.

patch   The patch on his shirt did not <u>match</u> the patch on his pants.

plan   Where do you plan to <u>plant</u> the garden?

rode   We rode very slowly over the bumpy <u>road</u>.

wrote   Who wrote the song, "On the <u>Road</u> to Mandalay"?

ill   The man was too ill to climb the <u>hill</u>.

rice   We hear that the price of rice will <u>rise</u> two cents a pound.

where   Where can I find a hard<u>ware</u> store?

pour   Please pour <u>more</u> cream into the pitcher.

boys   Do you think that boys have more <u>poise</u> than girls?

Mike   We gave Mike a <u>bike</u> for his birthday.

baby   We will name the baby after her Aunt <u>Mamie</u>.

cat   The cat did not care for <u>canned</u> food.

signed   I signed my initials on the back <u>side</u> of the paper.

tap   The tap on the door disturbed my <u>nap</u>.

think   I could not think of a <u>thing</u> to say.

I   I have something in my <u>eye</u>.

threw   Who threw the ball <u>through</u> the window?

knows   No one knows how the boy broke his <u>nose</u>.

sail   My sail boat will be up for <u>sale</u> next spring.

DESCRIPTIVE DEVICE--WHO IS THIS MAN?

Procedure: First read sentence by sentence with class participation.
Then re-read for thought and to increase attention span.

He was brought up in extreme poverty.
He did not even finish grade school.
His father died when he was only thirteen years old.
The family were so poor that they could not afford a coffin.
Friends chipped in and paid for the coffin.
After the father's death his mother had to work harder than ever.
She worked ten hours a day, six days a week.
This poverty began to worry the boy.
He wanted to get away from it all.
To escape the poverty he became interested in amateur theatricals.
These plays were put on by his church.
He had a natural talent for acting.
This led him into public speaking and then into politics.
At the age of 30 he ran for state legislature.
He was elected but he was not prepared for the job.
The bills and papers he was supposed to read were all Greek to him.
He was made a member of the State Banking Commission.
This was terrible.
He had never even had a bank account in his whole life.
To make matters worse he was appointed to a committee on forests.
As a city boy he had never been in a forest.
He was so discouraged that he wanted to resign.
He would have, except that he was ashamed to admit defeat to his mother.
So he set out on a course of self-education.
For the next few years he studied and read for sixteen hours a day.
He became the greatest living authority on the government of his state.
He had never finished grade school, but he picked up degrees from six
    universities.
He was elected Governor of his state.
He served as Governor for four terms.
Then he ran for the Presidency, but he lost.
Even though he was defeated he was one of the most beloved citizens
    to ever run for that office.
Do you know who he is?
His name is Al Smith.
(He died in 1944.)

LESSON 12--INITIAL AND FINAL L

Description: For "L" the tip of the tongue goes up behind the front teeth.
It is a very visible movement.

VOCABULARY

labor	loganberry
low	livelihood
lily	call
library	wall
little	table
label	apple

1. Who was the first woman Secretary of Labor?
2. The Labor Department will release the figures on unemployment.

1. We visited the low lands of Scotland.
2. There are very few mountains in the lowlands.

1. The yellow lily has large blossoms.
2. The lily of the valley has small flowers but large leaves.

1. You will find many of Jefferson's letters in the Library of Congress.
2. In what year was the Library of Congress built?

1. The label says wash in warm water.
2. The label on the bottle was marked "poison."

1. Where does the loganberry grow?
2. The loganberry is a cross between the raspberry and the blackberry.

1. How did your grandfather make his livelihood?
2. Abe Lincoln made his livelihood as a lawyer.

1. Please call the office and ask for the manager.
2. Why did you call off the meeting?

1. How much did you pay for the wall-to-wall carpeting?
2. Please do not push the chair too near the wall.

1. The table was set for breakfast.
2. This drop-leaf table is an antique.

1. The winesap is a tart apple.
2. My grandmother made delicious apple butter.

1. Please give me just a little more time.
2. A big brother will always protect his little sister.

HOMOPHENES

Directions: Write one word from each group on the blackboard.

lambs   What is the difference between lamb's wool and the
                    wool of the llama?
               The street lamps in the small town were old-fashioned.
               The cat makes a strange sound as it laps its milk.

lump   The artist works with a lump of clay.
               Who was Abner in the Lum and Abner radio program?

limp   The lettuce leaves were wilted and limp.
               A squirrel was playing on the limb of the tree.

lone   Who is the Lone Star Ranger?
               Do you know how to load a gun?
               The bank will be glad to give you a loan.

leak   There is a leak in the water main.
               Do you follow Little League baseball?
               This leek is delicious.

bail   The bail was set for five thousand dollars.
               How much does the bale of hay weigh?
               The robin's egg is a pale blue.
               Our mail comes at nine o'clock every morning.
               What is the difference in color in the male thrush
                    and the female thrush?

vowel   We cannot spell a word without using a vowel.
               The rooster is a large fowl.
               The umpire called "foul ball."

sail   The blue boat has a white sail.
               The clerk failed to make a sale.

mole   Do you believe that the mole is blind?
               This old bowl was found in an Egyptian tomb.
               The fishing pole was long and slender.
               Do you have any faith in the Gallop Poll?

DESCRIPTIVE DEVICE--LANDMARKS

Procedure: Read for thought.

This is an old church.
This church is in the State of New York.
The church was built in 1697.
The church has been in continuous use except during the American Revolution.
This is the Old Dutch Church of Sleepy Hollow.

This is a landmark over 100 years old.
This landmark is in one of the southern states.
This landmark was built in 1857.
It was used as the sign of a tinsmith's shop.
This is the Big Coffee Pot of Winston Salem, North Carolina.

This is an old landmark in Massachusetts.
This landmark was made in 1775.
This is the statue of a man named Captain Parker.
This statue is in honor of the Minutemen who gathered on the Green
    to oppose the British.

This landmark is in one of the southern states.
This is a statue of an Indian chief.
He was Chief Paduke of the Chickasaw tribe.
General William Clark named the city of Paducah after this friendly Indian.

This landmark can be seen in Fort Worth, Texas.
It is the statue of a cowboy riding his horse into the sunset.
The statue was dedicated by General Eisenhower in 1947.
A sign on the statue reads "The World's Most Beloved Cowboy--Will Rogers."

This landmark is a large stone.
This stone is in a cemetery.
There is the face of a man on the stone.
The stone reads: "I would rather be a servant in the house of the Lord
    than to sit in the seat of the mighty."
Alben Barkley, 1956.

This is another old landmark.
This is in a large city on the west coast.
This landmark moves--it runs on cables.
This landmark goes up and down hills.
It rides many people every day.
This is the famous San Francisco cable car.

LESSON 13--T

Description: For the formation of T, the tongue goes to the back
               of the roof of the mouth. Difficult to see at times.

VOCABULARY

tea	time
tie	temperature
tell	terms
table	tailor
take	tennis
taste	tooth

1. The tea plant has white flowers.
2. The tea plant grows in China and Japan.

1. This accident will tie up traffic.
2. Can you tie a lover's knot?

1. Can you tell the difference between salt and white pepper?
2. Some people just cannot tell the truth.

1. The table cloth was made of Irish linen.
2. Please do not spill punch on the lace table cloth.

1. Who will take the minutes of the meeting?
2. The secretary will take six weeks' leave of absence.

1. This salad has a taste of garlic in it.
2. Will you taste this sauce and see if it is too tart?

1. Some people are always behind time in their work.
2. We will make changes in the plans from time to time.

1. What is a person's normal temperature?
2. Have you ever tried to take a patient's temperature?

1. Those two men have not been on speaking terms for three months.
2. The terms of the contract may be changed if necessary.

1. The tailor will finish the suit on Friday.
2. This suit was made by a tailor in Hong Kong.

1. Have you ever watched Bobby Riggs play tennis?
2. Australia is well known for its tennis champions.

1. Do you have a tooth ache?
2. The dentist will remove the wisdom tooth.

HOMOPHENES

Procedure: Write one word from each group on the blackboard.

tab   Who will pick up the tab for lunch?
Ruby Keeler is an excellent tap dancer.
You will feel better after you have had a nap.
You must never try to nab a bone away from a dog.
The basement was damp after the rain storm.
There was a dab of grease on the seat of the chair.
Who is the engineer in charge of building the dam?

tack   Please tack the notice on the bulletin board.
She has the knack of making people feel at ease.
That old horse is just a nag.
The blue tag on the dress means a size twelve.

tail   The cheetah has a long tail.
This is a tale of the South Pacific.
Where did you find the rusty nail?
The hospital was located in a dale.

tan   That tan shirt is very becoming to you.
The reporter's name was Dan Rather.
My grandmother will show you how to tat.
Nan is the nickname for Nancy.
My mother and dad have moved to Florida.
The gnat was flying around the lamp light.

DESCRIPTIVE DEVICE

Procedure: Read for thought.

This is a city.
It is a large city.
This is a seaport city.
It is located on Puget Sound.
This is in the State of Washington.
This is Tacoma, Washington.

This is a man.
He was born in Ohio.
He was a very important man.
He died in 1930.
He was the 27th President of the United States.
He was a chief justice of the Supreme Court.
This is William Howard Taft.

This is a place.
It is a beautiful island.
It is one of the Society islands.
It is famous for its beautiful women.
This is Tahiti.

This is a tree.
It is a large tree.
It grows in East India.
The tree has white flowers.
The wood of the tree is used for shipbuilding.
This is a teakwood tree.

This is a city.
It is a large city.
This city is on the Mediterranean Sea.
It is in Israel.
This is Tel Aviv.

This is a river.
It is a large river.
It flows into the Mediterranean Sea.
It flows through Rome.
It is in Italy.
This is the Tiber River.

This is a city.
It is a large city.
It is in the south.
It is in the northern part of Florida.
It is the capital of Florida.
This is Tallahassee.

This is a spider.
This spider lives in Europe.
It is also found in the southern part of the United States.
It is a large, hairy spider.
It is poisonous.
This is a tarantula.

This is a leaf.
This leaf comes from a common plant.
It comes from the aster plant.
The leaves of the plant are very fragrant.
The leaves are used for seasoning.
This is the tarragon.

This is a city.
It is a large city.
It is on the Wabash River.
It is in the western part of Indiana.
This is Terre Haute.

This is a river.
This is a well-known river.
It is in the southern part of England.
This river flows through London.
This river flows into the North Sea.
This is the Thames River.

This is a plant.
It belongs to a poisonous family.
The flowers may be pink or white.
The leaves are very large.
The leaves are used for making cigarettes.
This is the tobacco plant.

LESSON 14--D

Description: For "D" the tongue goes to the back of the roof of the mouth. Difficult to be seen at times.

VOCABULARY

dream	debt
dime	deep
day	deer
doctor	dove
dark	district
dollar	dozen
door	drug

1. Do you dream every night?
2. Have you ever dreamed that someone was chasing you?

1. What can you buy for a dime?
2. Please give me a dime for a phone call.

1. The part-time employee will work a three-day week.
2. On what day of the week were you born?

1. Who was George Washington's family doctor?
2. One of the men who signed the Declaration of Independence was a doctor.

1. Some people prefer the dark meat of the turkey.
2. Some of the leaves are dark green and some are brown.

1. What is the size of a dollar bill?
2. The cab fare was one dollar and twenty-five cents.

1. Have you ever been caught in a revolving door?
2. The doors of the Cathedral were made of wood and bronze.

1. How long did it take to repay the debt?
2. The interest on the debt is paid quarterly.

1. The man has a deep bass voice.
2. I was deep in thought when you spoke to me.

1. We saw many deer in the national park.
2. The deer came up to the cabin to be fed.

1. The dove has soft gray feathers.
2. Why is the dove the symbol of peace?

1. How many hospitals are there in the District of Columbia?
2. Is there much unemployment in the District of Columbia?

1. We buy our sheets and towels by the dozen.
2. We will need two dozen rolls for the party.

1. Would you like some information about drug abuse?
2. There is an interesting pamphlet on dangerous drugs.

HOMOPHENES

Procedure: Write one word from each group on the blackboard.

dare
Where was Virginia Dare born?
Please do not <u>tear</u> the page out of the book.
The <u>tare</u> is a poisonous weed.

dart
I saw the child dart behind the car.
The <u>tart</u> was filled with blueberry jam.
A small mountain stream is called a <u>tarn</u>.

den
We keep our TV set in the den.
Will you <u>tend</u> to this assignment for me?
What were the <u>net</u> proceeds of the sale?
Please call me before <u>ten</u> tomorrow night.
We can pay off the <u>debt</u> in five years.

mud
The receding flood water left much mud.
<u>Mutt</u> and Jeff are very old comic strip friends.
The clove is the <u>bud</u> of a flower.
Would you like another cinnamon <u>bun</u>?
We heard the <u>putt</u> <u>putt</u> of the outdoor motor.
Have you ever seen a goat <u>butt</u> his head against a fence?
A <u>pun</u> is a play on words.

DESCRIPTIVE DEVICE

Procedure: Read for thought.

This is a dog.
He is a large dog.
He is a large, lean dog.
He has short hair.
He is black and white.
He has been called a coach dog.
This is a Dalmatian.

This is a man.
He lived a long time ago.
He had a very narrow escape.
He was thrown into the lions' den.
He was Daniel.

This is something small.
It has a sharp point.
It can be used in a game.
It can be used in hunting.
This is a dart.

This is a place.
It is a very dry place.
It is a very hot place.
It is in Eastern California.
It is 276 feet below sea level.
This is Death Valley.

This is a plant.
It grows low on the ground.
It spoils the lawn.
But it has a pretty yellow flower.
This is a dandelion.

This is a city.
It is a large city.
It is in southwest Ohio.
This city is on the Miami River.
This is Dayton, Ohio.

This is a woman.
She was a very beautiful woman.
She is mentioned in the Bible.
She was a friend of Samson.
Her name was Delilah.

This is a small cube.
It can be made of plastic.
It can be made of bone.
It is marked on each side with dots.
These are used in games of chance.
This is dice.

This belongs to the whale family.
It is a mammal.
It has a beaklike snout.
It can be trained to perform.
This is a dolphin.

This is a bird.
It was a large bird.
Sometimes it was called a stupid bird.
Its home was on an island in the Indian Ocean.
It is now extinct.
It had large wings.
But it could not fly.
This is a dodo.

LESSON 15--INITIAL N

Description: "N" is a nasal sound. For N the flat edge of the tongue
            goes toward the back roof of the mouth.

VOCABULARY

name	newspaper
know	nothing
nephew	need
number	note
knew	nurse
neighbor	news
notice	noise

1. What is the name of the town we just passed through?
2. Do you have a nickname?

1. We never know when we may have to work overtime.
2. Do you know why the paper boy was late this morning?

1. How long has your nephew worked at the White House?
2. Do you know my nephew's name?

1. I remember the name of the street but not the house number.
2. The phone company gave me an unlisted number.

1. We knew by the tone of his voice that he was angry.
2. I knew I had said the wrong thing.

1. Have you met your new neighbor?
2. My neighbor is never at home on the weekends.

1. Did you notice the name on the office door?
2. The postman left a notice for me to pick up a package at the
   post office.

1. The Boy Scouts collect old newspapers once a month.
2. There is a stack of old newspapers in our basement.

1. Nothing was said about their change of plans.
2. I have nothing interesting to read this evening.

1. Do you need anything more before I leave?
2. You will need some new clothes if you plan on going on a
   winter cruise.

1. Will you please give this note to the hotel clerk?
2. Who gave you the box of scented note paper?

1. My doctor has a new nurse.
2. I will speak to the nurse about a change in your diet.

1. I wish someone would tell me some good news.
2. I do not believe all the news I read in the paper.

1. The noise gave me a headache.
2. We must learn to put the noise in the background.

HOMOPHENES

Procedure: Write one word from each group on the blackboard.

niece
My niece will be twenty-one in June.
My knees were stiff from climbing the stairs.

nut
If you will crack the nuts I will make some candy.
What have you done to your hearing aid?

noise
The noise of the plane wakened me.
The firemen will repair the toys for the poor children.

name
Smith is an old family name.
The guest speaker was a Colonial Dame.
Why must there be so much red tape involved?
The policeman grabbed the thief by the nape of the neck.

near
Do you live near your office?
Have you ever sent a letter to Dear Abbey?
The cold wind brought a tear to my eye.
Will you show me how to cook deer meat?

no
Some people say no when they mean yes.
We never know what will happen tomorrow.
Who stepped on my toe in the dark?
Have you ever eaten sour dough biscuits?
The tow boat was causing a commotion on the river.
Have you ever seen a wild doe in the woods?

DESCRIPTIVE DEVICE

Procedure: Read for thought.

This is a small town.
This town is in the region of Galilee.
It is 20 miles from the Mediterranean Sea.
It is 70 miles from Bethlehem.
This is the home town of a very famous man.   Nazareth

This is a state.
It is one of the west north central states.
It is bounded on the south by Kansas.
It is 415 miles wide.
It is 205 miles long.
It comes from an Indian word meaning "flat water."   Nebraska

This is a man.
He was a friend of Ghandi.
His father was a wealthy lawyer.
He was well liked by his people.
He was the first Prime Minister of independent India.
His first name means "red jewel."   Nehru

This is a gas.
It was discovered in 1898.
It was discovered by a British chemist.
This gas is found in the atmosphere in very small portions.
It is one part gas to 55,000 parts air.
This gas is colorless.
This gas is odorless.   Neon

This is a country.
It is a country in Western Europe.
It is bounded on the west and north by the North Sea.
This country covers 15,000 square miles.
The name of this country means "woodland."
The capital is Amsterdam.
This place is sometimes called Holland.   Netherlands

This is a state.
It is one of the mountain states.
It is 484 miles long.
It is 322 miles wide.
The name of this state is a Spanish word.
The word means "snow-capped."   Nevada

This is a drug.
The drug is used for local anesthesia.
It is absorbed very quickly into the blood stream.
It loses its effect quickly.
The dentist uses this drug.   Novocain

This is a state.
It is one of the New England states.
It is one of the 13 original states.
It is a densely wooded state.
No part of this state is far from the water.
The seacoast of this state extends 18 miles along the
    Atlantic Ocean.   New Hampshire

This is a state.
It is one of the southwestern states.
It has a very dry climate.
The Rio Grande River is the principal river of this state.
The state ranks first in the production of uranium.   New Mexico

These are symbols.
The Egyptians used these many years ago.
They had their own set of symbols.
Their symbol for 100 was a chain.
Their symbol for 1000 was a lotus flower.
Their symbol for 10,000 was a pointed finger.
Their symbol for 100,000 was a tadpole.
These symbols were their ....   Numerals

This is a state.
It is one of our south Atlantic states.
It is a very wide state.
It is 503 miles wide.
It is 187 miles long.
This is the third largest state east of the Mississippi River.
It is one of the thirteen original states.
It is an agricultural state.   North Carolina

LESSON 16--FINAL N, T, D

Description: Tongue goes to roof of mouth. Difficult to see.

VOCABULARY

seen
moon
plain
sign
clown
brain
born

red
wide
wood
cat
wait
shout
fought

1. Have you seen the latest play at the National Theater?
2. I am sure I have seen that man before.

1. There will be an eclipse of the moon tonight.
2. How far is it from earth to the moon?

1. The room was plain but very cheerful.
2. Please give me just a plain ham sandwich.

1. There was no sign of rain when we left home.
2. There was little sign of life in the city over the weekend.

1. The clown made all the children laugh.
2. The clown rode the elephant in the parade.

1. You must use your eyes as well as your brain.
2. Do you believe that fish is a good brain food?

1. Herbert Hoover was born on a farm in Iowa.
2. She was born with a silver spoon in her mouth.

1. Did you notice how red the moon looked last night?
2. There is an old red farmhouse at the top of the hill.

1. How wide is the mouth of the Amazon River?
2. There is a wide difference in their ages.

1. Will you help me polish the hardwood floor?
2. The wood of the holly tree is as white as ivory.

1. The cat was asleep in the window in the sunshine.
2. Do you believe a cat has nine lives?

1. It is not worthwhile to wait any longer.
2. I will wait for you at the post office.

1. We heard them shout to us as we passed by.
2. A shout of laughter came through the window.

1. My grandfather fought in the Civil War.
2. The battle was fought long and hard.

HOMOPHENES

Procedure: Write one word from each group on the blackboard.

been   Where have you been since the last time I saw you?
            The farmer kept the apples in a bin in the cellar.
            How much will you bid for this rare piece of china?
            I bit my tongue while eating a piece of candy.
            My grandmother raised mint in her garden.
            The diamond pin was very expensive.
            The President pinned a medal on the soldier.
            The hunters dug a pit to trap the elephant.

did   We did not have time to finish our shopping.
            I could hardly hear above the din of the machinery.
            Shall I knit you a pair of wool socks?
            There was a rosy tint to the sky this morning.

DESCRIPTIVE DEVICE--FROM RAGS TO RICHES

Procedure: Read through sentence by sentence.   Then read as a
             whole for thought.

This man was one of eleven children.
He was number seven in line.
The family were very poor.
They lived on an island.
The father earned twelve dollars a month working in a sugar cane field.
Everyone in the family had to pitch in and help support the family.
When this little fellow was four years old he had a job.
He was a bean picker and earned thirty cents a day.
Some of his other jobs, later on in life, included being a shoe shine
  boy, a news boy, a golf caddie, and a crab digger.
He managed to go to school and graduate.
After he graduated from high school he wanted to go to a university.
He worked three years to save enough money to enter the university.
While he was in college he had a part-time job collecting bills.
He was a very smart boy.
He graduated from college in three years.

This was the wrong time to enter the business world.
The Depression had hit.
But he found jobs to help him save for his next goal.
He wanted to attend Harvard Law School.
He had a difficult time getting into Harvard.
His undergraduate degree was not from an accredited university.
But Harvard finally accepted him on one condition.
He must remain in the upper tenth of his class.
He did.
In 1930 he had his law degree and three thousand dollars in school debts.
Within the next few years he cleared his debt and saved five hundred
    dollars.
He put the five hundred dollars into a business venture with some
    friends.
The business failed but it taught him a lesson.
He then joined a law firm.
He was a major in the Air Force in World War II.
In 1952 he went into another business venture.
He and ten other friends invested 25,000 dollars each in a loan
    corporation.
The corporation was called Finance Factors.
Today the firm is worth 12 million dollars.
He was always interested in politics.
In 1952 and 1956 he served as a delegate to the Republican National
    Convention.
In 1959 he became a senator from his state.
He is well known and well liked.
He has three homes--two in Honolulu, including a cattle ranch, and
    one home in Bethesda, Maryland.
This is Senator Hiram Fong of Hawaii.

LESSON 17--HARD C

Description: Hard "C," like "K," is formed in the throat and is almost impossible to see.

VOCABULARY

come	car
call	cause
coffee	company
color	corner
copy	Canasta
cake	Canary
cook	Commander
candy	corporation

1. Please come one half hour early so we can have a talk.
2. If you come by way of the Beltway you will save time.

1. We make all our long-distance calls in the evening.
2. The long-distance call between Colorado and California was not as expensive as expected.

1. Do you like Taster's Choice coffee?
2. The coffee bean is a small brown bean.

1. Did Grandma Moses paint with oil or water color?
2. The snow scene in water color won first prize.

1. Where did you find that old copy of the Constitution?
2. Will you make a copy of this recipe for me?

1. This pound cake is rich but delicious.
2. Please put an extra cake of soap in your traveling bag.

1. Why do some men like to cook?
2. This is my favorite casserole cookbook.

1. This tastes like homemade candy.
2. Do you like peppermint stick candy?

1. Do you drive a company car?
2. The car skidded on the wet road and turned completely around.

1. Sometimes I think welfare is a lost cause.
2. We did not know what was the cause of the fight.

1. We are expecting more company over the holidays.
2. We will have still more company when we move into our new house.

1. The date on the cornerstone says 1713.
2. When was the cornerstone of the Library of Congress laid?

1. The Canasta game lasted three hours.
2. Have you ever played Canasta with five decks of cards?

1. Where are the Canary Islands?
2. The Canary Islands are off the coast of Africa.

1. The Company Commander was well liked by all of his men.
2. Commander Jones will retire at the end of the month.

1. General Motors is one of our larger corporations.
2. Which corporation showed the largest profit at the end of the year?

HOMOPHENES

Procedure: Write one word from each group on the blackboard.

cape
How many people are employed at Cape Canaveral?
We <u>came</u> home by way of Chicago.
We all know that we cannot win every <u>game</u>.

cab
What time did you tell the cab driver to come?
Would you like to send a boy to <u>camp</u> this summer?
Where is the <u>cap</u> to the tube of toothpaste?

could
Could I speak to you for a moment?
This is as <u>good</u> a time as any to break the news.

card
The top card is the Ace of Spades.
Please be on your <u>guard</u> when you take the dog for a walk.

creep
I did not hear the boy creep up behind me.
Please put <u>cream</u> but no sugar in my coffee.

Colonel
When did Colonel Lindbergh cross the Atlantic?
The milk will <u>curdle</u> if heated too fast.
A <u>kernel</u> of corn popped out of the popper.

cramp
What should you do if you have a cramp while swimming?
Shall we serve cole slaw with the <u>crab</u> cakes?
Does a <u>gram</u> weigh more than a dram?

crowd
The crowd went wild when our team won the game.
Are you sure this coffee is freshly <u>ground</u>?
This <u>crown</u>-of-thorns plant belongs to the cactus family.

DESCRIPTIVE DEVICE

Procedure: These paragraphs are read sentence by sentence, then
             re-read as a whole for thought.

This is a woman.
She was born in England in 1875.
She died in 1915.
She was an English nurse in World War I.
She was in charge of a hospital in Brussels.
She was there when the German troops occupied the city.
She helped about 200 soldiers to escape.
She helped them to escape to the Dutch border.
She was finally arrested.
She was sentenced to die.
She went before a German firing squad.
Her last words were: "Patriotism is not enough."
Her name is Edith Cavell.

This is a woman.
She was born in a small town in the United States.
She was born in Springfield, Pennsylvania, in 1907.
She was a biologist.
She was also a science writer.
She worked most of her life with the United States Wildlife Service.
In 1951 she wrote a book.
This was the story of the ocean.
The book was called "The Sea Around Us."
But her most popular book was published in 1962.
In this book she warned us about the use of insecticides.
This book was "Silent Spring."
Her name is Rachel Carson.

This is a woman.
She was a nurse.
She was an American nurse working in Havana, Cuba.
The time was in the year 1903.
She was working with a team of doctors.
The doctors were American doctors and Cuban doctors.
They were working with yellow fever victims.
They needed proof of an experiment.
This woman offered to be a guinea pig.
She volunteered to be bitten by the mosquitoes.
She caught the yellow fever.
She died from yellow fever.
But her sacrifice was not in vain.
The doctors, through her, were successful in almost entirely
   eliminating yellow fever.
Her name is Clara Moss.

LESSON 18--K AND HARD G

Description: Both of these are formed in the throat and are almost impossible to see.

VOCABULARY

keep	grade
keen	grand
ketchup	grow
key	game
Kodak	give
kind	girl
go	garage

1. Sometimes it is very difficult to keep a secret.
2. Do you always keep your promise?

1. My dog has a keen sense of hearing.
2. Most birds have keen eyesight.

1. Do you use ketchup or lemon on your fish?
2. This is a bottle of homemade ketchup.

1. Have you an extra front door key?
2. I have lost the key to my briefcase.

1. This Kodak takes very good pictures.
2. What size film do you use in your Kodak?

1. Our new neighbors are a kind, middle-aged couple.
2. Please tell me what kind of party you have in mind.

1. Shall we go to the concert this evening?
2. We plan to go to Idaho for the month of May.

1. Why is Grade A beef so expensive?
2. What is the highest grade you have ever made in mathematics?

1. We have grandstand seats at the ball park.
2. There is a Safeway and a Grand Union grocery in my neighborhood.

1. The sunflower grows by the wayside.
2. Those weeds may grow to be three feet tall.

1. Shall we play a game of pinochle?
2. I would rather play a game of gin rummy.

1. What shall we give Carl for his birthday?
2. I would like to give Carl a new billfold.

1. The girl has a very friendly personality.
2. Which one of the girls looks like her mother?

1. We parked the car in the garage.
2. The garage mechanic will check the oil for you.

HOMOPHENES

Procedure: Write one word from each group on the blackboard.

good
    We received a good price for the property.
    We could not stand the suspense any longer.

gave
    Who gave you that information?
    The Dead Sea Scrolls were found in a cave.

gum
    Do you know how chewing gum is made?
    The cup was made of fine bone china.
    My little brother is a Cub Scout.
    Would you like to come to dinner with us?

gap
    Where is the Delaware Water Gap?
    His father is a cab driver.
    We pitched our camp by the side of the lake.
    Would you rather wear a cap or a hat in cold weather?

gift
    That is a very expensive gift.
    Will you please give me a hand with this heavy box?

grew
    The boy grew to be as tall as his grandfather.
    How many men are there in the ship's crew?

grape
    Have you ever eaten wild grape jelly?
    The crepe myrtle has a beautiful flower.

grow
    Does this plant grow well in the north?
    Where does the crow build his nest?

DESCRIPTIVE DEVICE--WHO IS THIS PERSON?

Procedure: Read sentence by sentence first. Then re-read for whole
thought.

This woman was born in New York State in 1860.

She was born on a farm.

She was one of ten children.

Her father was a farmer.

She had to help her brothers and sisters on the farm.

She did not have time to go to school.

She became a hired girl when she was 12 years old.

In 1887 she married a hired hand.

She was a very small, pretty girl.

She was now 27 years old.

She and her husband rented a farm in Virginia.

They worked hard.

They had a farm in the Shenandoah Valley.

She had ten children but only five lived.

In 1905 they moved back up north.

They went back to New York State.

Her husband died in 1927.

She was sad, but she said she had a very happy life.

She was now seventy years old.

She kept on farming to support herself.

But when she was seventy-eight, something happened to her.

She developed arthritis in her fingers.

Her hands became too crippled for farm work.

She took up a hobby.

She took up the hobby of oil painting.

She was on her way to twenty-one years of fame and fortune.

She had never visited an art gallery.

She had never had a painting lesson.

She copied from Currier and Ives prints.

Then she began to paint original farm scenes.

She wanted people to see how she used to live.

She had always been a keen observer.

She worked from memory.

Some of her paintings were shown at the Museum of Modern Art.

She was given the Women's National Press Club award.

She visited President Truman in the Blair House.

She asked him to play the piano for her, and he did.

In 1955 Ed Murrow interviewed her on television.

She even had a one-man art show in New York City.

In all she painted more than 1,600 pictures.

They were naive but individualistic.

She was called the Grand Old Lady of American Art.

This was Anna Mary Robertson Moses.

LESSON 19--DOUBLE CONSONANTS

PL, PR, BR, BL

Description: For P or B the lips come together. For R there is a
forward movement of the lips, and for L there is
the tongue movement. These are visible consonants.

VOCABULARY

played	brown
plot	bring
plan	brief
plumber	bridge
president	block
prime	blow
prepare	blank
private	blind

1. Bing Crosby played the part of a priest in the movie.
2. Have you ever played golf at Pebble Beach?

1. The plot to hijack the plane was discovered just in time.
2. Three men were in on the plot to rob the bank.

1. We always plan our menus one week in advance.
2. Do you plan to invite all of your friends to the party?

1. The plumber charges by the hour.
2. Sometimes the plumber charges more than the doctor.

1. President Johnson's brother has written a book about him.
2. The president of the company is a young man.

1. The new TV show will have prime time on Sunday night.
2. This restaurant specializes in prime roast of beef.

1. Who prepared your income tax for you?
2. The doctor is prepared for any emergency.

1. The sign says private property.
2. We will try to arrange for a private meeting with the president.

1. There are many brown stone houses in New York City.
2. Some nuts are dark brown and some nuts are light brown.

1. Please bring home some fresh fruit from the farm.
2. Come along and bring a friend with you.

1. The newspapers gave a brief account of the accident.
2. Do you always carry a briefcase with you?

1. How far is Natural Bridge from Washington, D.C.?
2. The traffic was heavy on Chesapeake Bay Bridge on Sunday night.

1. The Statler Hotel is one block from the White House.
2. The old courthouse still stands in the middle of the block.

1. One side of the page was blank.
2. I always carry a blank check in my wallet.

1. Ray Charles is a blind piano player.
2. Who is in charge of the Lighthouse for the Blind?

HOMOPHENES

Procedure: Write one word from each group on the blackboard.

plays   There are two very promising plays running on Broadway now.
        We watched as the sun went down in a <u>blaze</u> of glory.

prove   We will do all we can to prove his innocence.
        Do you have <u>proof</u> that you are right?

profit This is the smallest profit we have ever made.
        John the Baptist claimed to be a <u>prophet</u>.

proud   You have the right to be proud of your work.
        My dog is white with <u>brown</u> spots.

bright The bright light was shining in my eyes.
        Who is the author of <u>Pride</u> and Prejudice?

place   This is the place where we had lunch last week.
        Mary <u>plays</u> the organ for our church choir.

plan   Will you help me plan a surprise birthday party for
          the boss?
        I <u>planned</u> on going home for lunch, but I was too busy.
        Please keep this <u>plant</u> in the sunshine.
        The <u>plaid</u> jacket was made in Scotland.

plate   The plate broke into three pieces when it fell onto the floor.
        Why was the <u>plane</u> late?
        I like <u>plain</u> home-cooked meals.

DESCRIPTIVE DEVICE--PLEASANT MEMORIES

Procedure: Read first sentence by sentence. Then re-read as a whole
for thought.

This is the story of a woman.

Her first name was Marie.

Marie was born in France.

When Marie was six years old she was adopted by an uncle.

Her uncle had a museum.

Marie spent lots of time in the museum.

She loved to watch her uncle at work.

He taught her many secrets of his work.

In a few years she herself was quite good in his work.

Her uncle let her use some of her own ideas.

When Marie was 29 years old she went to the palace of Versailles.

She went to work for the Royal Family.

When the Revolution came she was thrown into prison.

Marie was made to work while she was in prison.

She had to make models of the heads of "the enemies of the people."

After the war was over she was released.

In the meantime her uncle had died and left her two museums.

He left her something else, also.

He left her a debt of 60,000 francs.

She had to pay off this debt before she was allowed to leave the city.

Marie married a Frenchman, but her marriage was not a success.

She decided to leave France and start over in England.

She took her models to London.

Everyone admired her work.

She worked for two years in London.

Then she decided to tour the country with her models.

The tour was supposed to last four years.

Instead it lasted over thirty years.

Everyone enjoyed her work.

She finally came back to London to work some more.

But she was 70 years old before she achieved her greatest ambition.

This was to have a permanent exhibition of her work.

Then the whole world could come to see it.

Her dream came true in 1835.

She opened her exhibit on Baker Street in London.

She continued to make models for another seven years.

Before she retired she made one more model--a very special model.

This was her own self-portrait in wax.

The last years of her life were her happiest.

She had a home across the street from the museum.

She loved to watch the crowds come to the museum.

She died in the spring of 1850.

Thousands of mourners lined up to pay their respects.

Madam Marie Tussaud had had a very successful life.

LESSON 20--FR, FL

Description: The lower lip touches upper teeth for F. Forward movement of lips for R, tongue movement for L. Both formations are visible.

VOCABULARY

fry	floor
free	flower
Friday	flight
front	flavor
fresh	flood
frown	flame
fruit	flow
friend	

1. I will fry the bacon while you make the coffee.
2. We are going to a fish fry on Friday night.

1. Who is the author of Born Free?
2. The animals were allowed to roam free through the park.

1. We will meet you on Friday at 4 o'clock.
2. My next appointment with the dentist is on Friday morning.

1. The front door is locked but the back door is open.
2. Please park the car in front of the house.

1. This fresh asparagus is delicious.
2. Shall we serve fresh fruit salad?

1. The bright sun makes me frown.
2. If you frown too much you will have wrinkles.

1. What is your favorite fruit?
2. This fruit cake is very rich.

1. I would like you to meet a friend of mine.
2. Thomas Jefferson was a friend of Patrick Henry.

1. The apartment has hardwood floors.
2. There are many strange plants on the floor of the ocean.

1. Have you ever seen this flower before?
2. Are you a flower child?

1. Did you have a good flight?
2. Our flight was 2 hours late.

1. The anise seed has a strange flavor.
2. A dash of curry will improve the flavor.

1. The heavy rains caused the flood.
2. Some streets flood every time we have a heavy rain.

1. The flame leaped out of the fireplace.
2. Some of the flames were three feet high.

1. The river flows through the valley.
2. The water flows quickly over the dam.

HOMOPHENES

Procedure: Write one word from each group on the blackboard.

float   We let the boat float down the stream.
            Have you ever <u>flown</u> over the Rockies?

flew   The sea gull flew close to the ship.
            There seems to be an epidemic of <u>flu</u> this spring.
            The swallows built a nest in the chimney <u>flue</u>.

flour   Do you use self-rising flour in the cake mix?
            I've never seen this <u>flower</u> before.

friend   What is your friend's name?
            Don't <u>fret</u>, I'll buy you another ice cream cone.
            Tom and <u>Fred</u> are twins.

Frank   His name is Franklin, but we call him Frank.
            The <u>franc</u> is a French coin.

flow   Do you believe water can flow up stream?
            The ship was damaged by the ice <u>floe</u>.

DESCRIPTIVE DEVICE--WHO IS THIS MAN?

Procedure: Read first sentence by sentence. Re-read as a whole for thought.

He was born in New York City in 1894.

He did not like school.

But he did complete the first year of high school.

Then he decided to waste no more time on formal education.

He wanted to go to art school.

He worked at odd jobs and saved his money.

Then he entered art school.

In fact, he signed up for two art schools.

He attended one art school in the morning.

And the other art school in the afternoon.

He was quite good.

Before long he was illustrating books.

He was drawing pictures for boys' magazines.

There was a certain warmth and humor about his pictures.

By this time he was 22 years old.

His first cover picture appeared on a magazine in 1916.

This was a cover for The Saturday Evening Post.

Since then he has painted 350 covers.

He has been painting for over 40 years.

His paintings have been enjoyed by more people than any other American
    artist.

He is called the world's most famous illustrator.

He is a sort of pictorial Mark Twain.

He is still painting at his home in Stockbridge, Massachusetts.

This is Norman Rockwell.

LESSON 21--TR, DR

Description: Tongue to roof of mouth for "D" or "T"--forward
movement of lips for "r"

VOCABULARY

try	dream
train	drive
traffic	drug
trial	draw
trouble	drawer
trip	drop

1. Did you try to win first prize?
2. If you try, I think you can persuade them to go with us.

1. The train leaves at eight o'clock on track nine.
2. Please come on the early train.

1. The traffic officer is a busy man.
2. The traffic is always heavy on a holiday.

1. The Smith case will go to trial next month.
2. You can read the report of the trial in the newspaper.

1. Don't look for trouble--trouble will look for you.
2. Please do not go to any trouble on my account.

1. We are planning a trip to Wyoming next fall.
2. Is this trip necessary?

1. What did you dream about last night?
2. I dream of Jeannie with the light brown hair.

1. Shall we drive home through the park?
2. We will drive to Detroit next week and bring home a new car.

1. There are many new drugs on the market.
2. Some drugs have bad side effects.

1. You may draw your own conclusions.
2. Will you draw up our agreement for me to sign?

1. You will find a stamp in my desk drawer.
2. The small drawer in my desk is thick and will not open.

1. I will drop you a line as soon as we have some definite news.
2. The room was so quiet you could hear a pin drop.

HOMOPHENES

Procedure: Write one word from each group on the blackboard.

dry   We will pack the medicine in dry ice.
              Please try not to go to sleep during the lecture.

trim   Someone ought to trim the hedge.
              The round trip ticket will cost forty dollars.
              Do you prefer drip coffee or percolated coffee?

trap   Where shall I set the mouse trap?
              The dog barked at the tramp.
              The room was drab and dreary.
              A dram is equal to one teaspoon.

truck   The produce was shipped by truck.
              Will you help me open this old trunk?

drew   We drew all of our savings out of the bank.
              These statements are either true or false.

drain   The plumber has come to fix the drain in the kitchen sink.
              The train travels at a hundred miles an hour.

A LIKELY LEGEND

Procedure: Read sentence by sentence for thought. Then re-read as a
                   paragraph for thought. (Helps to increase concentration span.)

This man was born somewhere in Massachusetts.

No one knows exactly where in Massachusetts.

He first appeared in the Ohio Valley in the year 1800.

He was a very odd sight.

He came out of the east.

He was barefoot.

His clothes were worn but clean.

He carried a Bible.

On his back he carried a pouch.

This pouch was filled with apple seeds.

He brought these seeds from western Pennsylvania.

He was always lighthearted and laughing.

He never seemed to suffer from cold or hunger.

He was deeply religious, and, he said, "He often talked with the angels."

He was welcomed everywhere by frontier families.

He would appear before a cottage with a small gift.

Sometimes it was a piece of cloth for the mother.

Sometimes it was a small toy for the child.

He would ask if he could spend the night.

He always slept on the cabin floor.

In the morning he would arise very early.

He would go out and plant a small grove of apple trees for his host.

He seldom accepted any money.

If he did, he spent the money on sick or wounded animals.

For nearly half a century he crisscrossed the American midwest.

He planted his apple seeds wherever he went.

He is believed to have died about 1847.

He died in Indiana.

But on March 22, 1847, there appeared an obituary in a newspaper.

The newspaper was the Fort Wayne <u>Sentinel</u>.

The obituary stated that: John Chapman died in March, 1845--
                         otherwise known as Johnny Appleseed.

LESSON 22--H AND VARIOUS VOWELS

Description: "H" has no formation of its own, but takes the form of the vowel that follows.

VOCABULARY

house   hospital
here   hundred
ham   harbor
horse   high
have   hat
help   hotel

1. How long have you lived in this house?
2. We bought this house for 35,000 dollars two years ago.

1. I will meet you here in one half hour.
2. Please be here at two o'clock sharp on Friday.

1. I would like a ham and cheese sandwich and a malted milk.
2. How much did you pay for the fifteen-pound ham?

1. What was the name of Paul Revere's horse?
2. A gray horse won the first and last race.

1. Have you been waiting very long?
2. We have been very busy at work all week.

1. I need all the help I can get if you want the job finished by
   5 o'clock.
2. My secretary will help you with the typing.

1. How many times have you been a patient in a hospital?
2. What is the correct address of the Washington Hospital Center?

1. How much did you pay for the hundred tickets to the ball game?
2. We need one hundred names on the list for it to be effective.

1. Do you remember Pearl Harbor?
2. There were seven ships in the harbor.

1. What is the highest point of land in Maryland?
2. There are many high-rise apartments in Silver Spring.

1. President Johnson hated to wear a hat.
2. Please put your hat and coat in the hall closet.

1. There are 144 rooms in this hotel.
2. We stay at the same hotel in Ocean City every summer.

HOMOPHENES

Procedure: Put one word from each group on the blackboard.

harm   No harm will come to you if you are careful.
            Please take hold of my <u>arm</u> when we cross the street.
            Not many musicians know how to play the <u>harp</u>.

here   Please meet me here on Friday afternoon.
            Do you know a good <u>ear</u> specialist?
            I can <u>hear</u> but I cannot understand what you say.

hill   Our house on the hill faces the ocean.
            She has been quite <u>ill</u> for a long time.

hat   Not many men like to wear a hat.
            Bob <u>and</u> Bill are brothers.
            Will you be <u>at</u> home this evening?
            Please <u>hand</u> me the paper.
            We saw <u>an</u> elephant and a zebra at the zoo.
            Will you <u>add</u> this column of figures for me?
            Have you <u>had</u> a busy day?
            How much <u>did</u> you pay for the <u>ad</u> in the Sunday paper?

DESCRIPTIVE DEVICE

Procedure: Read first for thought, then re-read as a whole.

1. This is an herb.
    It is a native of Europe.
    The plant has long leaves and a long root.
    The root is used for food.
    The root is made into a relish.
    The root is grated.
    It has a very biting taste.
    Some people like it and some do not.
    This is a horseradish.

2. This plant belongs to the mint family.
    It is common in Europe and Asia.
    It grows along the countryside.
    It also grows in North and South America.
    The plant grows three to five feet high.
    Many white hairs cover it.
    This gives the plant a whitish appearance.
    The flowers are small and almost white.
    The leaves and stem are used in making cough medicine.
    This is a horehound.

3. This is a tall hardy plant.
    It is native to Asia.
    But it is grown widely in the United States.
    It has large fuzzy leaves.
    It has a tall heavy stem.
    It blooms from July to September.
    The flowers are round and open.
    The flowers can be white, yellow, red, or purple.
    The plants are used as background borders for flower beds.
    Or they are planted along the fence.
    This is a hollyhock.

4. This is food.
    It is made from corn.
    The grains of corn are soaked in a weak lye solution.
    This causes the kernels to puff up.
    Then the kernels are washed well.
    They are now ready to be cooked.
    This is a favorite dish in the South.
    It may be boiled or fried.
    It is usually served with meat.
    This is hominy.

5. This is a land and water animal.
   It lives in the swamps.
   These swamps are in the tropics of Africa.
   Next to the elephant it is the heaviest of all mammals.
   Only two kinds of this animal live today.
   One weighs as much as 8,000 pounds.
   The other is a pygmy.
   This animal has a very thick skin.
   It has a barrel-shaped body.
   Its legs are short and thick.
   Its eyes and ears are very small.
   Its mouth is huge.
   It lives in a family group.
   This is a hippopotamus.

ALPHABETICAL LISTING
OF HOMOPHENOUS WORDS

On the following pages you will find an alphabetical
listing of homophenous words. This list has been
compiled at the request of my many lipreading pupils
who are amazed at the number of homophenous words
with which a lipreader has to contend.

This list is made without regard for long or short
vowels. You will also note that silent "K" words
are included in the K listing, and "CH" and "SH" words
follow in their regular order. It will be up to the
teachers to explain these formations.

This list is not perfect or complete, thus there is
room for additions. It is simply intended as an aid
and an incentive for teachers.

Mae T. Fisher, Audiologist
and Teacher of Lipreading

A

Abet, amend

About, abound, amount

Abuse, amuse

Act, hanged, hacked

Add, ad, had, at, hat, an, hand, and, ant, aunt

Adieu, ado

Advice, advise

Aid, ate, hate, eight

Ail, ale, hale, hail

Aim, ape, Abe

Air, hair, heir, ere, hare

Aisle, I'll, isle

All, hall, haul, awl

Allowed, aloud

Altar, alter

Am, ham

Analyst, annalist

Arc, ark, hark

Arm, harm, harp

Art, hard, heart, hart

Ascend, ascent, assent

Ash, hash

Assistance, assistants

Auger, augur

Aught, ought

Awful, offal

B

Bad, bat, ban, band, banned, mat, man, mad, manned, pan, pad, pat, pant, panned

Badge, Madge, patch, match, batch, mash

Bail, bale, pail, pale, mail, male

Bait, paid, bayed, pain, pane, pate, paint, pained, main, maid, made, mate, Maine, mane

Ballot, mallet, pallet, pallid

Balm, Bob, palm, pop, mob, mop, pomp

Bar, mar, par

Bare, bear, pair, pare, pear, mare, mayor

Barn, barred, bard, part, mart

Baron, barren

Base, bass, bays, maze, mace, maize, baize, pays, pace

Bass, mass, pass, Mass

Battle, pattle, paddle, mantel, mantle, panel, banal

Bay, May, may, pay

Beach, beech, peach

Bead, bean, beat, beet, mean, meat, meet, Pete, peat, mien

Beak, meek, peak, peek

Bed, bet, bent, bend, pen, pet, pent, pend, penned, met, meant, mend, men, Ben

Bee, be, pea, me

Beer, bier, mere, peer, pier

Bees, peace, peas, piece

Berry, bury, Perry, merry, Mary, marry

Berth, birth, mirth

B

Bide, bind, bite, mite, might, mind, mined, mine, pied, pint, pine, pined

Bill, pill, mill

Birch, perch, merge, purge

Bird, burn, burned, pert, purred

Black, blank, plank, plaque

Blade, plane, plate, played, plain, planed

Bland, plan, plant, plaid, plait

Blaze, place, plays

Blew, blue

Blight, blind, plied , plight

Bloc, block

Blonde, blot, plod, plot

Bloom, plume

Blush, plush, plunge

Board, bored, poured

Boat, bone, bode, moan, moaned, moat, mown, pone

Boast, post, most, posed

Boll, bowl, mole, pole, poll

Boon, boot, mute, booed, moon, mewed

Bore, more, pour, poor, boar, mower

Born, borne

Borough, burro, burrow

Bough, bow, mow

Boughs, mouse, bows

Bouillon, bullion

Braid, brain, prayed, preyed

B

Brake, break

Brand, brat, brad, Pratt, Brandt

Bray, pray, prey

Breach, breech, preach

Bread, bred

Brick, prick, bring, brink, prig, prink

Bridal, bridle

Bride, pride, bright, brine, pried

Brown, proud

Bounce, pounce, pounds, pouts, mounts, mounds, bounds

Buck, bug, bung, monk, mug, punk

Bunch, punch, munch, mush

Burs, purrs, purse, burse

Bustle, muscle, muzzle, mussel, puzzle

But, butt, mutt, put, pun, bun, punt, bud, mud, bundt

Buy, my, pie, by, bye

C

Cad, cat, can, cant, can't, canned, gad, gant

Call, gall, Gaul

Came, cape, game, gape

Canvas, canvass

Carat, carrot, caret, Karen

Card, cart, guard

Case, gaze

Catarrh, guitar

Cave, gave   79

Cease, seize, sees, seas

Ceiling, sealing

Cellar, seller

Censer, censor

Cent, sent, send, scent

Cession, session

Chap, jab, jamb, Jap, champ, sham

Char, jar

Cheer, jeer, sheer, shear

Chews, shoes, juice, choose, Jews

Chewed, chute, shoot, jute, June

Chip, ship, Jim, gym, gyp

Chum, chump, jump

Clad, clan, glad

Clam, clamp, clap

Clans, glands, glance

Class, glass

Clause, claws, gloss

Clean, cleaned, glean, gleaned, cleat

Cleans, gleans, cleats

Cleanse, glens

Climb, clime

Clip, glib

Clock, clog

Clothes, close

C

Cloud, clown, clout

Clue, glue

Coal, goal

Coarse, course

Coast, ghost

Coat, goat, cone, code, goad

Cob, gob

Cold, gold, colt

Colonel, kernel, girdle, curdle

Comb, cope

Core, corps, gore

Could, good

Council, counsel

Crab, cram, cramp, grab, gram, gramme, gramp

Crack, crag, crank

Crane, crate, grate, great, grade, grain

Craze, graze

Creak, creek, Greek

Cream, creep

Crease, grease

Creed, greed, green, greet, Crete

Crevasse, crevice

Crib, crimp, grim, grip

Cried, grind

Croup, group, groom

Crow, grow

C

Crowd, ground, crown, crowned, grout

Crutch, crunch, crush, grudge

Cup, come, gum, cub

Curl, girl

Currant, current

Cymbol, symbol, simple

D

Dab, dam, damp, nap, nab, tab, tam, tap, tamp, damn

Dale, tale, nail, tail

Dame, name, tape, tame, nape

Darn, tart, dart, tarn

Date, Dane, Dade, Nate, deign

Daunt, dawn, dawned, gnawed, naught, taught, taunt, taut

Dazzle, tassel

Dead, debt, den, dent, ten, tend, tent, net, Ned, Ted

Dean, deed, neat, need, knead, teen

Dear, deer, tear, tier, near

Deem, deep, team, teem

Descendant, descendent

Desert, dessert

Device, devise

Dew, due, do, to, too, two, new, knew, gnu

Did, din, dinned, dint, tin, tint, knit

Die, tie, dye, Nye, nigh

D

Died, night, dine, dyed, dined, knight, tide, tied, diet, tine, tight

Dim, dip, nip, tip, nib

Dime, time, type, thyme

Dish, ditch, niche, tinge

Dive, knife

Doe, toe, dough, no, know, tow

Done, dun, nun, nut, ton, dud, tun, tut

Doom, tomb, dupe

Door, tore, nor

Dose, doze, nose, toes, knows, does

Dot, don, tot, nod, not, knot, donned

Dote, known, note, tote, toad, tone, toned, towed, don't

Doubt, down, noun, town

Draft, draught

Dread, tread, trend, Trent

Drug, drunk, truck, trunk

Dual, duel

Dumb, dump, dub, tub, numb

E

Ear, hear, here, e'er

Eel, heel, heal

Either, ether

Elm, helm, help

Ere, air, hair, heir, hare

E

Ermine, Herman

Ethel, ethyl

Ewe, you, hew, hue

Ewes, hews, hues, use, yews

F

Fad, fan, van, vat, fat

Fade, fane, fate, faint, feigned, feign, fete, fain, vain, vein, vane, feint

Fair, fare

Fairy, ferry, very, vary

Falls, false

Fast, vast

Fay, fey

Fed, vet, fend, vend, vent

Feed, feet, feat

Few, view

Fib, vim

Final, vital, vinyl

Fine, vine, find, fined, fight

Fir, fur

First, verse

Firm, verb

Fits, fix

Flea, flee

Flew, flu, flue

F

Float, flowed, flown

Floe, flow

Fogs, fox

Fore, four

Forte, fort

Forth, fourth

Foul, fowl, vowel

Freeze, frieze, frees

Friend, fret, Fred

Fuse, views

G

Gab, cab, camp, gap

Gait, gate, Kate, gain, Cain, cane, Cade

Game, came, cape, gape

Gave, cave

Gaze, case

Geese, keys, quays

Ghost, coast

Gift, give

Gild, guilt, gilt, guild, killed, kiln, kilt

Girl, curl

Goal, coal

Goat, coat, cone, code, goad

Gold, cold, colt

G

Good, could

Grab, gram, gramp, crab, cramp, cram, gramme

Grace, graze, craze

Grand, grant

Grate, grade, great, crane, crate, grain

Greed, greet, green, Crete, creed

Grey, gray

Grim, grip, crib, crimp

Grind, cried

Groan, grown, crone

Ground, crowd, crown, crowned, groat

Grow, crow

Guessed, guest

Guide, kind, kite, kine

Gum, come, cup, cub

Gym, gyp, Jim, ship, chip

H

Had, hat, hand, ad, add, and, ant, aunt, at, an, Ann, Anne

Hail, hale, ail, ale

Ham, am, hap

Hare, ate, eight, ade, aid

Hear, here, ear, ere

Heard, herd, earn, hurt, urn

Heat, eat, heed, heet

H

Hers, hearse

Hoard, horde

Hoe, owe

Hoes, owes, hose

Home, hope

Honor, odder, otter, hotter

Hop, hob

Hot, odd

Hound, out

Hobo, oboe

Hide, height

High, eye, hi, I, aye

Him, hip, imp, hymn

Hitch, hinge, inch, itch

Hue, hew, you, ewe

I

I, eye, hi, aye, high

Ice, eyes

Ides, hides

Idle, idol, idyll

Ill, hill

I'll, isle, aisle

Imp, him, hymn, hip

Impen, impend

I

Inch, itch, hinge, hitch

Incidence, incidents

In, it, hit, hint, hid, id, inn

Incite, inside, insight

Indebted, indented

Infest, invest

Ingrain, ingrate

Intend, intent

Intern, inturn

Ire, hire

Is, his

J

Jab, jam, Jap, jamb

Jack, shack

Jar, char

Jeep, cheap, sheep

Jeer, cheer, sheer, shear

Jingle, shingle

Jim, gym, gyp, ship, chip

Job, shop, chop

Joe, show

Join, joint, joined

Juice, choose, shoes, Jews, chews

June, jute, shoot, chewed, chute

K

Kate, gate, gait, gain, cane, Cain, Cade

Kay, gay

Key, quay

Keys, geese, quays

Killed, kiln, kilt, gild, guild, gilt, guilt

Kite, kine, kind, kyte

Knack, nag, knag

Knap, nap, nab, tab, tap, tam, tamp, dam, damp, damn

Knave, nave

Knead, need, neat, neet, dean, deed

Knee, nee, tea, D, tee

Knell, Nell, dell, tell

Knelt, dealt

Knew, new, do, due, dew, to, too, two, gnu

Knife, dive

Knight, night, tight, tine, tied, dine, dined, died

Knob, nob, top, tom, knop

Knot, not, tot, Tod, nod, don

Know, no, dough, doe, toe, tow

Known, don't, tone, toned, towed, toad, tote, note, dote

Knows, nose, toes, does, tows

Knub, nub, numb, dump, dumb, tub, dub

Krone, crone, groan, grown, groat, growed, crowed

L

Lace, lays

89

L

Lack, lag, lank

Laid, lane, late, lain, layed

Lamb, lamp, lap, lab

Larch, large

Lath, lathe

Laud, lawn

Laugh, lave

Lea, lee

Lead, led, let, lent, lend

Lead, lean, leaned, lien

Leaf, lief, leave

Leak, leek, league

Leased, least

Lessen, lesson

Lewd, lute, loot, loon

Liar, lyre

Licence, license

Lie, lye

Lieu, loo

Limb, limp, lip, lib

Limber, lipper

Live, lift

Lion, line, light, lined

Load, loan, lode, lone, loaned

Loam, lobe, lope

L

Loom, loop, lube

Lose, loose

Lumber, lubber

Luck, lug, lung

M

Mace, baize, base, bass, bays, maize, maze, pace, pays

Mad, man, mat, bad, ban, bat, band, banned, pat, pant, pan, panned, pad

Made, maid, main, Maine, mane, pain, pate, pane, payed

Mail, male, pail, pale, bail, bale

Mall, ball, pall, maul, Paul

Mare, mayor, bear, bare, pear, pair, pare

Mark, bark, park, marque

Meal, peel, peal

Mean, mien, bean, beat, beet, bead, peat, Pete, meet, meat, mete

Mere, pier, bier, peer, beer

Merge, birch, perch, purge

Met, meant, men, mend, bet, bent, bend, Ben, pen, penned, pet, pent, pend

Might, mite, mine, mind, mined, bite, bight, bide, pine, pined, pint, pied

Missal, missile, mistle

Missed, mist

Moan, mode, bode, boat, bone, mote, moat, mowed, mown, moaned

Mob, mop, Bob, bomb, pop, pomp, palm, balm, mom

Monk, mug, bug, bunk, bung, pug, punk, buck, puck, muck

M

Most, post, boast

More, bore, pour, poor, boar, pore

Muscle, mussel, puzzle, bustle, muzzle

Must, bust, mussed, bussed

N

Nab, dab, tab, tamp, tam, dam, damp, damn, nap

Nags, tacks, tanks, tax, tags

Nail, dale, tail

Name, dame, tame, tape

Naught, taught, gnawed, dawn, dawned, daunt, taunt, taut

Naval, navel

Nay, day, neigh

Naze, daze, days, dais

Near, deer, dear, tear, tier

Neat, need, knead, dean, deed, neet

Net, ten, tend, tent, Ned, Ted, dent, debt, den, dead

New, knew, do, due, dew, to, too, two, gnu

News, deuce

Next, text, test

Nice, dice, dyes, dies

Niche, dish, ditch, tinge

Niece, tease, knees

Nigh, die, tie, dye

Nile, dial, tile

N

Nine, dine, tine, dined, tight, tide, tied, knight, dyed, died

Nip, dip, tip, nib, Tim, dim

No, know, doe, dough, toe, tow

Nock, dock, knock, tock

Nod, knot, not, tot, dot, don, non

Noise, toys

Nome, dome, tome

Nor, door, tore

Norm, dorm

Nose, dose, toes, knows, doze, tows

Note, dote, tote, known, tone, toned, towed, toad

Noun, down, town, doubt

Nude, dude, tune, noon, dune

Numb, dump, dumb, tub

Nun, nut, ton, tun, none, done, tut

Nurse, terse

Nuzzle, tussle

O

Oar, ore

Oat, owe, ode, owed, hoed

Obit, omit

Oboe, hobo

Odd, hot, hod

Offal, awful

O

Old, hold, Holt

Older, holder

Omen, open

One, won

Ooze, whose

Otter, hotter, odder, honor

Ought, aught

Our, hour

Out, hound

Owes, hose, hoes

P

Pace, mace, base, bass, maze, maize, baize, pays, bays

Pack, back, Mack, bag, bank, bang

Pad, mad, bad, band, banned, man, manned, mat, pat, pant, panned, bat

Paddle, battle, mantle, mantel

Paid, maid, made, payed, pain, paint, bane, bait, mate, main, Maine, pate,
    pane, bade, bayed

Pail, bail, bale, male, pale

Pair, pare, pear, mare, bare, bear, mayor

Pall, ball, mall, Paul

Pallet, mallet, palette

Palm, balm, Bob, mob, bomb, pomp, pop, mom

Pan, pand, pant, ban, band, bat, bad, man, mat, mad, pat, pad

Pang, bang

Paperback, paperbag

P

Par, bar, mar

Parch, march, marsh, barge, Marge

Park, bark, mark, marque

Parley, barley

Parry, marry, Barry

Part, mart, bard, barn

Pass, bass, mass

Passed, past, mast

Passive, massive

Paste, baste

Pastor, master

Patch, batch, match, Madge

Paten, patent

Path, bath, math

Patron, matron

Patten, patent, madden, batten, Patton

Pause, moss, boss

Pay, bay, may

Pea, be, bee, me

Peace, piece, peas, pease, bees

Peach, beech, beach

Pearl, burl, Merl

Peat, pean, meat, meet, mete, beat, beet, Pete, bean, bead, mean, mien

Pedal, pedale, petal, medal, meddle, metal, mental

Peddler, meddler

Peek, peak, pique, beak, meek

P

Peel, peal, meal

Peep, beep, beam

Peer, pier, mere, beer, bier

Peg, beg, Meg

Pell, bell, mell

Pelt, belt, melt, meld

Pen, pend, pet, pent, met, men, mend, meant, Ben, bend, bent, bet, bed

Penny, many, Benny

Pension, mention

Pepper, member

perch, birch, merge, purge

Perse, purse, burse

Pert, Bert, pern, burn, bird

Pest, best, messed

Petrel, petrol

Pew, mew

Pick, big, mink, pink, ming, pig, ping, Bing

Piddle, middle

Pie, by, my, bye

Pike, bike, Mike

Pile, bile, mile

Pill, bill, mill

Pillar, miller

Pillow, billow

Pin, pit, bin, bit, mid, Min, bid, mitt, mint

Pine, mine, mined, pint, mind, bind, pined

P

Pistil, pistol

Plan, plant, plaid, planned, plait

Plane, plate, planed, plain, played, blade

Plank, blank, plaque, black

Plays, place, blaze

Plied, plight, blight, blind

Plod, plot, blot, blonde

Plume, bloom

Plunge, plush, blush

Pod, pot, bond, mod, pond

Poise, boys

Point, poind

Pole, bole, mole, poll, boll

Pollan, pollen

Plot, bolt, molt, mold, mould, bold, poled

Pone, bone, moan, moat, bode, mode

Pony, bony

Praise, prays, preys, braise

Prate, prayed, braid, brain, brayed, preyed

Pray, bray, prey

President, precedent

Price, prize, pries

Prick, brick, brig, bring, prig, prink

Pride, bride, bright, brine, pried

Prince, prints

Principal, principle

P

Profit, prophet

Proud, brown

Prove, proof

Puck, buck, muck, pug, bung, bunk, mug, monk, bug

Pun, putt, punt, butt, but, bud, bun, bundt

Pump, bump, pup, mum, bum

Punch, bunch, munch

Purge, merge, birch, perch

Purr, burr, myrrh

Pus, bus

Puzzle, muzzle, bustle, muscle, mussel

Q

Quay, key

Quays, geese, keys

Quarts, quartz

R

Rabbit, rabid, rapid, rabbet

Race, raise, raze, rays

Rack, rank, rang, rag

Raid, rain, rein, rained, reined, reigned, reign, rate

Ram, rap, ramp, wrap

Ran, rant, rat, rand

Rapped, rapt, wrapped

R

Read, reed

Read, red, rent, rend, wren, redd, ret

Real, reel

Ream, reap

Rebound, remount

Recede, receipt

Reck, wreck

Redoubt, renown, redound

Reek, wreak

Rejoin, rejoint, rejoined

Relief, relieve

Reside, resign, recite

Reviews, refuse

Rhyme, ripe

Rice, rise

Ridge, rich

Rig, rink, ring

Right, rite, ride, Rhine, wright, write, rind

Rim, rip, rib

Road, rode, rowed, Rhone, rote, wrote

Roam, robe, rope, Rome

Role, roll

Root, rude, route

Round, route

Rum, rump, rub

Run, runt, rut

R

Rung, wrung, rug

Rye, wry

S

Sack, sag, sank, sang, sac

Safe, save

Sail, sale

Sap, Sam

Scull, skull

Sea, see

Seam, seem, seep

Sear, seer

Search, serge, surge

Seas, seize, cease

Seen, scene, cede, seat, seed

Serf, serve

Sew, so, sow

Shack, Jack, jag

Shade, Jane, chain, jade

Shale, jail

Sham, jam, jab, jamb

Shame, shape

Shard, chart, charred, chard, jarred

Share, chair

Sharp, charm

S

Shatter, chatter

Sheaf, chief

Shear, cheer, sheer, jeer

Sheath, sheathe

Sheen, sheet, cheat

Sheep, cheap, jeep

Shelf, shelve

Shell, jell

Sherry, cherry

Shilling, chilling

Shingle, jingle

Ship, chip, Jim, gyp, gym, shim

Shoe, chew, shoo, Jew

Shoes, choose, chews, Jews, juice

Shone, showed, shown, shoat

Shoot, June, chute, chewed

Shore, chore

Short, shorn

Shot, jot, John, shod

Shovel, shuffle

Shuck, chuck

Shudder, shutter

Shut, jut, shun

Sign, cite, site, sighed, sight, signed, side

Simple, symbol, cymbal

Sin, sit

S

Slab, slap, slam

Slay, sleigh

Sleight, slide, slight

Smoke, spoke

Smudge, sponge

Snare, stair, stare

Snob, stob, stomp, stop

Soar, sore

Sole, soul

Some, sub, sup, sum

Son, sun, sud

Spine, smite, spied, spite

Stab, stamp

Staid, stayed, state, stain, stained

Stair, stare

Stake, steak, snake

Steal, steel

Stud, stun, stunt, stunned

Stile, style

Straight, strayed, strait, strain, strained

Suite, sweet, Swede

Summer, supper

T

Tab, tap, tamp, tam, dam, damn, dab, damp, nab, nap

T

Tail, tale, nail, dale

Tame, dame, name, tape

Tart, tarn, dart, darn

Tassel, dazzle

Taught, taut, daunt, dawn, dawned, gnawed, naught, taunt

Tea, nee, D, tee

Team, teem, deep, deem

Tear, dear, deer, tier, near

Ten, tent, tend, net, Ned, den, dent, debt, dead

Than, that

Thawed, thought

Therefor, therefore

Thick, thing, think

Threw, through

Throat, throne, thrown

Tide, tied, tight, tine, nine, night, knight, dine, died, dined, dyed

Tie, die, dye, nigh

Time, dime, type, thyme

Timber, timbre

Tip, dip, nip, nib, Tim, dim

Tin, tint, did, dint, din, dinned, knit

Tinge, dish, ditch, niche

Toad, tone, dote, don't, tote, known, towed, note, node

To, too, two, new, knew, gnu, do, dew, due

Toe, doe, dough, no, know, tow

Toes, dose, doze, knows, nose, does

T

Tomb, doom, dupe, tube

Ton, done, dun, nut, tun, none, tut

Top, nob, knob, Tom

Tore, moor, nor

Tot, dot, Don, not, non, knot, nod

Town, down, noun, doubt

Toys, noise

Train, drain, trade, trait

Tramp, trap, dram, drab

Tread, dread, trend

Truck, drug, drunk, trunk

True, drew

Try, dry

Tub, dub, dumb, dump

Twin, twit

U

Udder, utter, under

Umbel, humble, Hummel

Up, hum, hump, hub, hup

Urn, earn, heard, herd, hurt

Use, ewes

V

Vail, fail, veil, vale

Vain, vane, fade, feign, feigned, faint, feint

Van, fan, fad, fat, vat

vault, fault

Veal, feel

Veer, fear

Vend, fend, fed, vent, vet

Verb, firm

Verse, first

Very, ferry, fairy, vary

Vial, file, vile, viol

View, few

Vim, fib

Vine, find, fine, fined

Vinyl, vital, final

Volley, folly

Vote, phone

Vowel, foul, fowl

W

Wade, weighed, wait, weight

Waist, waste

Waive, wave

Wad, want, what, watt, wand

Ware, wear, where

W

Warm, warp

Warn, ward, wart

Wash, watch

Way, weigh

We, wee

Weak, week

Wed, wen, wend, went, wet, when, whet

Were, whir

Whim, whip

Wide, wine, wind, white, whined, whine

Wig, Whig, wick, wink, wing

Wind, win, wit

Wish, which, witch

Won, one

wreath, wreathe

Y

Yam, yap

Yew, you, ewe, hue, hew

Yews, use, ewes, hues, hews

Z

Zoo, sue